The Future Has Already Happened

Gen AI and the New World Order

Tim Heaton
April 2024
All Rights Reserved

Table of Contents

Introduction 1
   Deciphering AI, ML, and GenAI: A Guide 3
   Part I: Work in the Age of Generative AI 5
      Chapter 1: Collaborative Dynamics Redefined 5
      Chapter 2: Careers on the Precipice 8
         Consultants 8
         Freelancers: Navigating the GenAI Revolution 9
         Customer and Technical Support Professionals 11
         STEM Educators, Cultivating Lifelong Learning 13
         Content Distribution, Beyond the Gatekeepers 14
         The Inevitable Transition 18
      Chapter 3: Occupations Growing in Attractiveness 19
         AI and Machine Learning Specialists: The Vanguard of the Technological Revolution 19
         Data Scientists and Analysts: Navigating the Data Deluge 21
         Digital Content Creators: Fueling the Digital Economy 23
         Healthcare Professionals: Expanding the Spectrum of Care 25
         Educational Technologists and Online Learning Specialists: Shaping the Future of Education 26
         Supply Chain and Logistics Specialists: Navigating Global Complexities 28
         Sustainability Experts: Eco-Conscious Business Practices 30
         User Experience (UX)/User Interface (UI) Designers: Crafting the Digital Frontier 32
         Cybersecurity Experts 34

Chapter 4: Emerging Occupations 38

    AI Ethicist: Navigating the Moral Landscape of AI 38

    Virtual Reality Experience Creators: Shaping Immersive Realities 40

    Urban Agriculture Specialists: Cultivating Green Spaces in the Concrete Jungle 41

    Quantum Computing Researchers and Engineers: Pioneering the Quantum Frontier 43

    Personal Privacy Advisors: Guardians of the Digital Self 45

    Genomic Counselors and Generative AI: Shaping the Future of Personalized Medicine 47

    Automation Integration Specialists: Harmonizing Technology with Human Workforce 49

    E-sports Professionals and Managers: Thriving in the Competitive Gaming Boom 50

    Content Creators: Harnessing GenAI for Creative Evolution 52

Chapter 5: Charting the Uncharted: GenAI's Revelation of the Unknown 55

    Conclusion: A New Era of Discovery and the Role of GenAI 59

Part II: Education Not Certification 61

Chapter 6: Introduction to STEAM: Embracing the Arts in the Age of GenAI 61

    Back to the Classics, Integrating Classical Wisdom 63

    Ethics: The Foundation of Innovation 63

    Psychology and Cognitive Science: Understanding the Human Element 63

    Leadership Skills: Guiding Technological Progress 64

    Philosophy: The Bedrock of Critical Thinking 64

    Summary 64

Chapter 7: The Evolution of Learning with GenAI 67
Personalization at Scale 67
Transforming Learning Methodologies 69
Beyond the Classroom: Lifelong Learning 72
Democratizing Education 74
Ethical and Practical Considerations 77
Consequences 81

Chapter 8: A New Paradigm, Holistic Knowledge Validation 85
Personalized Learning Pathways 85
Dynamic Skill and Knowledge Validation with GenAI 87
Continuous Feedback and Growth with GenAI 89
The Digital Portfolio: An Immutable Ledger of Achievement 91
Authenticating Holistic Knowledge 93
Conclusion of Chapter 10: A New Paradigm, Holistic Knowledge Validation 95

Part III: Economic and Social Impacts 97

Chapter 9: The New Economic Landscape 97
AI as the Cartographer of Knowledge 97
Transforming Legal Scholarship and Practice 99
Catalyzing New Research Directions 102
Publishers, Researchers, and Fact-Checkers: Embracing AI's Revelations 104
Revolutionizing Patent Searches 106
Reconfiguring Productivity 108
Transforming the Job Market 109
Redefining the Concept of Work 109

Navigating the Transition 110
Conclusion 110
Chapter 10: The GenAI Era, cutting through the complexity of Cross Disciplinary Discoveries. 112
Biomimicry and Materials Science 112
Environmental Science and Urban Planning 114
Impact on Urban Development 116
Neuroscience and Artificial Intelligence 117
Archaeology and Material Engineering 119
Astronomy and Pharmaceutical Research 122
Conclusion 124
Chapter 11: The GenAI Documentation Revolution 126
Healthcare and Medical Research: Enhancing Documentation Practices 128
Legal and Regulatory Compliance: Enhancing Documentation Practices 131
Education and E-Learning 133
Leveraging Synthetic Data for Enhanced Documentation 136
Chapter 12: Society Transformed 140
The Advent of AI-Augmented Direct Democracy 140
Potentialities Unleashed 140
Challenges to Navigate 141
Toward a Harmonized Future 141
The Privacy Conundrum 142
Navigating Ethical Dilemmas 143
Bridging the Digital Divide 143

The Path Forward 143

Summary 144

Part IV: A New World Order: GenAI Ethics and Governance. 145

Chapter 13: The Current State of GenAI Ethics and Governance 145

Chapter 14: GenAI self Governance: Using AI to Mitigate Human Bias with Traditional Cultural Foundations 158

Limitations of Humanistic Approaches to Ethics: 159

Transcendent Principles Discussed 160

Introduction to AI-Generated Transcendent Ethics and Rules 167

Part V : Quantum Computing 190

Chapter 15: The Infinite Frontier: Quantum Computing and GenAI 190

A Brief Explanation of Quantum Computing 190

Understanding Superposition in Quantum Computing 190

Quantum Computing and GenAI: Redefining Foundations of Discovery 192

Beyond Binary: The Quantum Leap 192

Generative AI and Multidimensional Analysis 192

Creating Foundations for Cross-Domain Discoveries 193

A New Era of Cognitive Exploration 195

Chapter 16: A New Era or the Final Chapter? 197

Quantum Artificial Life: Bridging GenAI and Quantum Computing 197

Enhancing Life Simulations with Quantum Capabilities 197

Ethical and Philosophical Implications 198

Then, What is Life? 199

Consciousness and Sentience 199

Ethical Considerations of Creating and Interacting with Artificial Life 200

Responsibility Towards Our Creations 200

Rethinking Our Place in the Universe 201

Theoretical Limits 201

Quantum Decoherence and Error Rates 201

Qubit Coherence Time 202

Scalability Challenges 202

Quantum Algorithm Limits 202

Fundamental Quantum Mechanics 203

Ethical Implications 203

Privacy and Data Security 203

Surveillance and Bias 204

Employment and Societal Impact 204

Dual Use and Weaponization 204

Long-term Societal Changes 205

Ethical AI Governance Using GenAI 205

The Responsibility of Harnessing GenAI 205

A Collaborative Path Forward 206

Conclusion for this Book 207

Appendices 209

Appendix A: Glossary of Terms Used in the Book 210

Appendix B: Resources for Further Exploration 214

AI Journals: 217

Quantum Computing Journals: 218

Online Courses: 218

Introduction

At the dawn of the 21st century, we stand on the precipice of a technological revolution poised to redefine our interaction with the world. Central to this revolution is Generative Artificial Intelligence (GenAI), a burgeoning field that melds creativity with computing power to push the boundaries of what machines can accomplish.

GenAI represents more than just a technological advancement; it embodies our intrinsic desire to innovate and expand our understanding of the world. This new era of artificial intelligence promises to unlock unprecedented levels of creativity and efficiency, with potential applications that stretch from the arts to the sciences. Imagine machines composing symphonies that move us, creating visual art that challenges our perceptions, and writing stories that captivate the imagination. Beyond artistic expression, GenAI's scope extends into practical realms such as personalized healthcare, where it can design treatments tailored to individual genetic profiles, and environmental management, where it can model complex climate scenarios and propose solutions to our most pressing challenges.

The integration of GenAI with quantum computing introduces a transformative synergy, catapulting computational capabilities to once-unimaginable heights. This fusion enables us to tackle complex problems across various domains—from decoding the intricate patterns of the human genome to exploring the vast mysteries of the universe—efforts that would have taken centuries with traditional computing methods.

This book ventures deep into the transformative potential of GenAI, amplified by the power of quantum computing. We will explore how this alliance is reshaping industries, revolutionizing economies, and altering the societal fabric, all while navigating the complex ethical landscapes that arise when creative power is handed over to machines.

As we embark on this journey through the GenAI revolution, this book aims not only to inform but also to inspire. It addresses critical questions about the responsible harnessing of this formidable technology: How do we ensure that our pursuit of technological advancement does not overshadow our ethical responsibilities? How do we mold a future that leverages these powerful tools while preserving the core of our humanity?

Join me in exploring the nexus of imagination and innovation that GenAI represents, where the future is not a distant dream but a new reality waiting to be shaped.

Tim Heaton

Deciphering AI, ML, and GenAI: A Guide

Understanding the nuances between Artificial Intelligence (AI), Machine Learning (ML), and GenAI is essential for anyone looking to grasp the current and future landscapes of digital innovation. Let's unravel these complex yet fascinating concepts to uncover the essence of each.

Artificial Intelligence (AKA, the Codex)

AI represents the broadest spectrum of computer science aimed at simulating human intelligence. It encompasses a diverse array of technologies and methodologies capable of tasks such as reasoning, learning, perceiving, problem-solving, and understanding language. From simple rule-based algorithms and decision trees to sophisticated neural networks, AI's versatility allows it to perform tasks that traditionally require human intellect.

Machine Learning (AKA, the Analyst)

ML, a critical subset of AI, empowers algorithms to learn from data and make predictions or decisions. This branch diverges from conventional AI by relying on statistical methods to enable machines to enhance their performance with experience. ML's realm is categorized into supervised learning, unsupervised learning, and reinforcement learning, each with distinct applications ranging from predictive analytics in finance to recommendation systems in entertainment.

Generative AI (AKA, the Savant)

GenAI narrows the focus further to the generation of new data that mirrors but is distinct from its training data. This field includes the creation of text, images, music, and other media, embodying a form of creativity. Technologies like Generative Adversarial Networks (GANs) and Variational Autoencoders (VAEs) are at the forefront of GenAI, with OpenAI's GPT series being a notable example in text generation, illustrating the creative potential of AI.

Navigating the Differences

Scope: AI acts as the umbrella under which all computational intelligence falls, ML specializes in data-driven learning, and GenAI focuses on the creation of novel content.

Functionality: While AI systems mimic human cognitive functions across a wide spectrum, ML systems concentrate on deriving insights and improving from data without explicit programming. GenAI pushes boundaries further by not only learning from data but also using it to create entirely new, unseen outputs.

Applications: AI's applications are vast, extending beyond learning tasks to include pre-programmed operations like chatbot responses. ML excels in areas requiring adaptive learning and improvement, such as spam detection. GenAI, however, thrives in creative arenas, generating realistic and original content, from artworks to literary compositions.

By these distinctions, we gain a deeper appreciation for the layers of innovation shaping our digital world. Each field, with its specific focus, contributes uniquely to the technological tapestry, driving us towards a future where the potential for invention and discovery is boundless.

Part I: Work in the Age of Generative AI

Chapter 1: Collaborative Dynamics Redefined

In the evolving landscape of work, the emergence of GenAI heralds a pivotal shift in collaborative efforts. This transformation, set against the backdrop of traditional online collaboration tools, fundamentally redefines teamwork and creativity paradigms. GenAI, a subset of artificial intelligence focused on generating novel data and solutions, extends beyond enhancing processes; it revolutionizes how we conceptualize, execute, and value collaboration.

The Advent of GenAI in Collaboration

Transitioning to GenAI-driven models signifies a move away from conventional tools that supported communication, document sharing, and project management. GenAI imbues collaborative work with a dynamic layer of intelligence, offering not just streamlined workflows but the ability to generate ideas, propose solutions, and predict project outcomes. This evolution from facilitative to generative technologies blends human intuition with AI's analytical prowess, exemplified by platforms like TensorFlow and GPT-3, which facilitate more nuanced and productive collaboration.

Transforming Teamwork

GenAI seamlessly integrates into teams, assuming a role akin to a quasi-member with unparalleled capabilities. It aids in drafting project outlines based on objectives and suggesting creative alternatives, previously unconsidered by human team members. In design projects, for example, GenAI's ability to quickly generate multiple prototypes tailored to varying criteria significantly accelerates the conceptual phase, allowing teams to focus on refinement and execution.

Enhancing Creative Processes

The profound impact of GenAI on creativity democratizes the creative process. Tools like DALL-E and AIVA provide individuals with the means to simulate the expertise of seasoned professionals, thus lowering entry barriers to creative fields. This technological advancement doesn't replace human creativity; instead, it amplifies it by removing routine barriers and fostering novel idea exploration.

The Role of Data and Feedback

A vital aspect of GenAI-driven collaboration is its reliance on vast datasets and continuous feedback, which ensures the system's effectiveness grows over time, adapting to the team's specific preferences and working styles. The feedback loop between human inputs and GenAI outputs creates a dynamic environment where both parties learn from each other, culminating in outcomes that surpass individual contributions.

Navigating the Challenges

Despite its promising potential, the transition to GenAI-driven collaboration presents challenges, including data privacy concerns, intellectual property issues, and the risk of over-reliance on AI solutions. Addressing these challenges requires developing new skills and adapting to new collaborative methods that prioritize communication, critical thinking, and the ability to work synergistically with AI.

Summary

The evolution from traditional collaboration tools to GenAI-driven models ushers in a new era of work, blurring the boundaries between human and machine capabilities and fostering a more dynamic collaboration form. As we embrace these changes, we stand at the threshold of a future where teamwork is not only more efficient but also more imaginative and inclusive. This journey into the redefined landscape of work invites us to reconsider our collective creative potential, with GenAI serving as both a catalyst and a companion.

Chapter 2: Careers on the Precipice

In the rapidly evolving landscape of GenAI, traditional careers such as consultants, freelancers, customer and technical support professionals, and even educators in STEM fields find themselves at a crossroads. The advent of GenAI challenges the future relevance of these professions, sparking a significant transformation that blends disruption with opportunity.

Consultants

"GenAI-powered language models allow users to access and process information on a vast scale, making it easier to stay informed on complex topics." - Lex Fridman, AI researcher.

With GenAI, everyone is an expert. This might sound ridiculous unless you've never paid a freshly minted MBA to advise you on your multinational company. The traditional role of the human consultant is undergoing a dramatic transformation because the cumulative data generated in today's digital age far exceeds the processing capabilities of any individual consultant. Even now, human consultants are struggling to keep pace, rendering traditional consultancy models increasingly obsolete. Firms renowned for their advisory services, such as Deloitte, Ernst & Young, KPMG, and PwC, are experiencing a paradigm shift, evidenced by significant personnel reductions.

This shift signifies not the diminishment of expertise but its democratization. GenAI, with its unparalleled data processing capabilities, has become the "all-knowing advisor," capable of synthesizing vast datasets to provide predictive insights and strategic guidance at a speed and scale unimaginable for human consultants alone. This is not just a change; it's a fundamental redefinition of what it means to be an expert.

Consulting firms, once reliant on the human capital of their highly skilled consultants, are pivoting to embrace the efficiency and effectiveness of GenAI. This transition is driven by the recognition that the volume and complexity of data now integral to strategic decision-making are far beyond human capacity to analyze without technological augmentation. The result is they just aren't needed.

Implications for the Consulting Industry

Job Market Evolution: The consulting industry must adapt to this changing landscape, where traditional roles are being reimagined. New hires must now bring skills complementary to AI, such as emotional intelligence, ethical judgment, and creative problem-solving, to interpret and implement AI-driven insights effectively.

Skill Set Shift: The skill set valued in consultants is shifting from purely analytical capabilities to include mastery in managing AI tools, interpreting their output, and leveraging these insights in strategic planning and decision-making processes.

Client Expectations: As clients become more aware of the capabilities of GenAI, their expectations from consulting firms are evolving. They no longer seek just advice but actionable insights derived from deep data analysis that only AI can provide at such scale and speed.

Ethical and Strategic Consideration: With AI taking on a more central role in consultancy, ethical considerations around data use, privacy, and decision-making transparency become increasingly critical. Firms must navigate these challenges carefully to maintain trust and ensure the responsible use of AI in their advisory roles.

Freelancers: Navigating the GenAI Revolution

"Some routine tasks currently handled by freelancers might become automated by AI. However, this could also create new opportunities for freelancers who specialize in working with or customizing AI tools, or who

focus on tasks requiring human creativity and emotional intelligence that AI struggles with." Andrew Ng

The freelance landscape is undergoing a seismic shift, thanks to the advent of GenAI. Traditionally valued for their niche expertise, freelancers are now at a juncture where the ability to adapt and integrate GenAI into their repertoire will define their success. The era of freelancers thriving as "one-trick ponies" is fading, giving way to a new breed of multi-faceted professionals who leverage GenAI to expand their service offerings.

GenAI's proficiency in autonomously executing a range of tasks—from crafting compelling content to developing software—presents a dual-edged sword. While it challenges freelancers to redefine their value proposition, it also unlocks unprecedented opportunities. The successful freelancers of tomorrow will be those who embrace GenAI not as a competitor but as a collaborator. They will harness its capabilities to diversify their skills, engage in a broader spectrum of projects, and deliver solutions that blend human creativity with AI efficiency.

Cultural Understanding and Creativity at the Fore

In the GenAI-enhanced future, freelancers will distinguish themselves through cultural understanding and creativity—attributes uniquely human and currently beyond the reach of AI. Cultural understanding enables freelancers to produce work that resonates on a global scale, navigating nuances and sensitivities that GenAI alone cannot comprehend. Creativity, too, remains a distinctly human forte, with freelancers leveraging GenAI to push the boundaries of innovation, be it in design, writing, or strategic thinking.

Integrating GenAI into the Freelance Workflow

The integration of GenAI into freelance workflows signifies a paradigm shift in how projects are conceptualized and executed. Freelancers will use GenAI tools to automate the routine and data-intensive aspects of their work, freeing up valuable time to focus on creative and strategic endeavors. This integration allows for an elevation in the quality of output, as freelancers can dedicate more resources to the conceptual and innovative aspects of their projects.

By incorporating GenAI, freelancers can also offer more competitive services, tapping into analytics and data-driven insights to inform their strategies and creative direction. This not only enhances the efficacy of their solutions but also positions them as forward-thinking professionals capable of leveraging the latest technologies to deliver superior results.

The Human-Centric Approach

Despite the technological advancements, the heart of freelance success in the GenAI era lies in the human-centric approach. Empathy, emotional intelligence, and a deep understanding of human desires and motivations will become the cornerstone of freelance work. These elements ensure that, regardless of how advanced GenAI becomes, the essence of freelance contributions—personal touch, understanding, and creativity—remains irreplaceable.

Customer and Technical Support Professionals

"Many customer service jobs involving routine inquiries and troubleshooting could be automated by AI chatbots and virtual assistants." Martin Ford (Author of "Rise of the Robots")

The landscape of customer and technical support will undergo significant transformation, propelled by the advancements in GenAI. Traditionally viewed as entry-level roles or stepping stones within the industry, the perception and reality of customer and technical support professions are shifting. While it has been challenging to progress beyond support roles, mainly due to the specialized skills and dedication required, GenAI is set to redefine this trajectory.

GenAI's capabilities extend far into understanding and navigating the complexities of technical documentation and user inquiries. This technological evolution means that support roles are no longer about merely guiding users through troubleshooting steps. Instead, these roles are evolving into sophisticated positions that leverage GenAI to interpret error messages directly, offer precise solutions, and enhance the overall user experience.

The Evolution of Support Documentation

In the age of GenAI, support documentation is transformed. Traditionally dense and labyrinthine manuals will become dynamically navigable resources. GenAI algorithms excel at parsing these documents, understanding their intricacies, and even updating them in real-time as new solutions are found. This marks a significant shift from passive repositories of information to active, learning databases that grow and evolve based on real-world interactions and solutions.

This capability doesn't just streamline the process of finding information; it revolutionizes it. Support professionals, armed with GenAI tools, can address user concerns with unprecedented accuracy and speed. The technology is adept at learning from each interaction, enhancing its database with every problem solved, making the next solution even more accessible and accurate.

The Future of Support Roles

The role of customer and technical support professionals is on the cusp of evolution. Far from being a niche or temporary position, the integration of GenAI into support functions elevates these roles to critical components of product development and customer satisfaction strategies. As products and services become more complex, the demand for skilled professionals who can leverage AI tools to provide exceptional support will only increase.

GenAI not only makes support more efficient but also more strategic. Support professionals will need to adapt, gaining skills in managing and working alongside AI to deliver solutions. This shift presents an opportunity for those in support roles to redefine their career paths, moving from traditional support to roles that blend technical expertise with strategic insight into customer experience and product improvement.

STEM Educators, Cultivating Lifelong Learning

"STEM education needs to go beyond technical skills. It's also about fostering collaboration, communication, and critical thinking. These well-rounded skills are essential for success in any field." Gwynne Shotwell (President and COO of SpaceX

The integration of GenAI into STEM education not only transforms pedagogical practices but also underscores a universal truth: we are all lifelong learners. This paradigm shift emphasizes that learning extends far beyond the traditional classroom setting and into the expanse of our entire lives. As educators transition from being the sole providers of knowledge to facilitators of learning, they instill in students the understanding that education is an ongoing journey, not a destination.

Embracing Continuous Learning
In this new educational landscape, the emphasis on teaching students how to learn becomes a cornerstone for developing lifelong learners. By leveraging GenAI, educators equip students with the skills to self-direct their learning, fostering a mindset of curiosity and an appetite for discovery that persists throughout their lives. This approach prepares individuals not only for the careers of today but also for the challenges and opportunities of the future, many of which are yet to be defined.

The Role of Educators
Educators themselves embody the principle of lifelong learning. As they adapt to the evolving demands of teaching in a GenAI-enhanced

environment, they continually acquire new skills, explore innovative teaching methodologies, and refine their understanding of how technology can augment learning. This commitment to professional and personal growth serves as a model for students, reinforcing the message that learning is a perpetual process enriched by exploration and adaptation.

Fostering a Culture of Continuous Improvement

The integration of GenAI in STEM subjects further catalyzes the shift towards a culture of continuous improvement. Students learn to view every project, experiment, and inquiry as a step in their learning journey, with each success and setback contributing to their growth. This perspective encourages resilience, adaptability, and a proactive stance towards lifelong learning, qualities essential for navigating the complexities of the modern world.

Everyone as a Lifelong Learner

Acknowledging that everyone is a lifelong learner reshapes our collective approach to education, career development, and personal growth. It dismantles the barriers between 'student' and 'professional,' 'teacher' and 'learner,' highlighting that we are all simultaneously teachers and students in different contexts of our lives. In a world where the only constant is change, embracing lifelong learning becomes our most reliable strategy for success and fulfillment.

Content Distribution, Beyond the Gatekeepers

There's a potential concern of AI-generated content flooding the market, raising questions about originality and the role of human authors." - Aisha Khan (Literary Agent)

The ascendancy of GenAI in the literary and publishing world heralds a sea change, challenging the traditional paradigms that have long dictated the flow of literary content to audiences. Historically, traditional content distribution channels have acted as gatekeepers, with editors, publishers, and literary agents determining which manuscripts make it to the public eye and which do not. This model, while having curated much of the world's celebrated literature, has also been critiqued for its exclusivity. The tale of J.K. Rowling's numerous rejections before the success of the "Harry Potter" series is a testament to the arduous path many authors face. It raises a poignant question: How many unique voices have we missed because they didn't persevere through countless rejections?

GenAI: Democratizing Literary Creation and Distribution

With the integration of GenAI into content creation and distribution, the landscape is shifting dramatically. GenAI is dismantling the traditional barriers to entry, democratizing the process of publishing. Authors no longer need to endure the often disheartening process of submitting manuscripts to multiple gatekeepers, only to face rejection. Instead, GenAI technologies enable authors to find their niche audience and publish their work directly, sometimes within the span of a single day. This rapid turnaround from creation to publication is not just a testament to efficiency but also to the potential for a more inclusive literary world.

The New Paradigm: Personalization and Niche Publishing

GenAI empowers authors to explore and cater to niche markets with unprecedented precision. By analyzing reading trends and preferences, GenAI can guide authors in tailoring their narratives to meet the specific tastes of virtually any reader group. This level of personalization was unthinkable in the traditional publishing model, where broad market appeal often trumped unique, niche storytelling. Furthermore, GenAI's capabilities extend to editing, formatting, and even marketing, providing a comprehensive suite of tools that supports authors from manuscript to market.

Challenges and Opportunities

This transformation is not without its challenges. The proliferation of content facilitated by GenAI raises questions about quality control, copyright, and the potential for oversaturation. However, it also presents opportunities for a more dynamic literary ecosystem, one where diversity of voice and story is the norm, not the exception. Authors who might have been overlooked by traditional publishers now have the chance to share their stories, contributing to a richer, more varied cultural tapestry.

The rise of GenAI in the literary and publishing sectors is recalibrating the balance of power, shifting control from traditional gatekeepers to the creators themselves. This shift promises a more equitable platform for authors, where determination and creativity, rather than access and approval, dictate who gets to share their story with the world. As we navigate this new landscape, the potential for discovery is limitless, with every day offering the possibility for new voices to be heard and new stories to be told.

Editors

In the editing domain, the prowess of GenAI has not just reached but surpassed that of human editors. GenAI brings to the table unparalleled efficiency in language correction, enhancing style, and executing structural edits swiftly and affordably. Its relentless evolution, fueled by extensive databases of literary content, has enabled it to exceed human capabilities in spotting inaccuracies, refining text, and maintaining consistency across documents. This technological leap positions GenAI as the preferred choice for authors and publishing houses, signaling a transformative shift in the editorial landscape where the traditional role of human editors becomes increasingly obsolete.

Copywriters

GenAI transforms stakeholders into direct creators, enabling them to produce engaging, effective content without traditional barriers. With GenAI tools at their disposal, stakeholders can instantly generate persuasive copy that resonates with their audience, eliminating the need for continuous back-and-forth edits. This efficiency revolutionizes the content creation process, as producing new, tailored copy takes mere seconds, vastly outpacing the conventional method of revisions and approvals. GenAI not only streamlines content production but also democratizes it, allowing stakeholders to directly shape their messaging with precision and speed.

Publicists

Publicity campaigns, traditionally dependent on the nuanced understanding of human publicists regarding media landscapes and personal networks, are undergoing a significant transformation. The emergence of GenAI solutions, armed with sophisticated Graph database technology, is at the forefront of this change. These technologies are adept at identifying incredibly specific audience segments for precise content targeting. This shift moves us away from the conventional reliance on the extensive knowledge and networks of human publicists.

GenAI's proficiency in analyzing media trends, predicting audience reactions, and automating social media interactions is revolutionizing the field of publicity. These technological advancements are diminishing the need for human involvement in everyday tasks, shifting the role of publicists towards more strategic and high-level planning. As GenAI's sophistication grows in crafting narratives that resonate with targeted demographics, it redefines the core responsibilities and skills of a publicist.

The incorporation of GenAI into publicity campaigns significantly increases both the accuracy and the impact of these efforts, marking the dawn of a new era where AI's analytical and predictive capabilities become the cornerstone of public relations strategies. This evolution underscores a pivotal transition in the industry, emphasizing data-driven insights and precision in reaching and engaging audiences.

The Inevitable Transition

The transformation within the literary and publishing industry towards GenAI is a vivid illustration of wider shifts occurring across various sectors, emphasizing a collective movement towards enhanced efficiency, scalability, and the ability to deliver highly personalized content. As GenAI technologies evolve to offer even more profound economic and operational benefits, stakeholders in the realms of editorial, copywriting, publicity, and publishing are increasingly favoring AI-driven methodologies.

This evolution into a future shaped by GenAI extends beyond mere adaptation; it demands a fundamental reconsideration of professional roles. The forthcoming landscape, deeply influenced by the capabilities of GenAI, challenges traditional norms and opens up new frontiers for content distribution. In this context, the innate human attributes of creativity, empathy, and ethical discernment rise to prominence, distinguishing human contributions in an ecosystem where AI plays a central role.

Professionals navigating this shift are called to not only adapt to but also thrive within this GenAI-integrated future. Success in this era is defined by the ability to synergize with AI, harnessing its strengths to amplify the uniquely human aspects of storytelling, emotional connection, and moral reasoning. As we step into this redefined world of content creation and distribution, the fusion of human insight with AI's analytical prowess heralds a new chapter of innovation and inclusivity in how stories are told and shared.

Chapter 3: Occupations Growing in Attractiveness

As we navigate through the transformative landscape ushered in by GenAI, certain professions are emerging as particularly crucial. Among these, the role of AI and Machine Learning Specialists stands out, with its importance magnified by the pervasive integration of AI across multiple sectors.

AI and Machine Learning Specialists: The Vanguard of the Technological Revolution

"As AI applications become more sophisticated, the need for specialists who can develop, maintain, and ensure the responsible use of these technologies will only increase." - Dr. Fei-Fei Li (Co-Director of the Stanford Human-Centered AI Institute)

The Why: A Convergence of Necessity and Innovation

Ubiquitous AI Integration: AI's centrality in modern industries is undeniable. From healthcare diagnostics to financial forecasting, AI technologies are becoming integral components of operational frameworks, driving efficiency, accuracy, and innovation. This widespread adoption has escalated the demand for specialists who not only understand AI and machine learning (ML) technologies but can also tailor these solutions to meet the specific needs of different sectors.

Complexity and Specialization: As AI technologies evolve, so does their complexity. Developing, managing, and implementing AI algorithms and ML models require a deep understanding of both theoretical foundations and practical applications. Specialists in this field must navigate the intricate landscape of neural networks, deep learning, and algorithm optimization, ensuring that AI solutions are both effective and ethical.

Innovation and Competitive Edge: In an increasingly competitive global market, businesses and organizations are seeking to leverage AI for strategic advantage. AI and ML Specialists play a pivotal role in driving innovation, identifying opportunities for AI integration that can transform business operations, enhance customer experiences, and open new avenues for growth.

Ethical and Responsible AI Use: With great power comes great responsibility. The expanding capabilities of AI systems have raised ethical concerns, from data privacy to algorithmic bias. Specialists in AI and ML are at the forefront of addressing these challenges, ensuring that AI technologies are developed and used in ways that are transparent, fair, and beneficial to society.

The Attractiveness of the Role

The growing attractiveness of careers as AI and ML Specialists is a reflection of both the demand for these skills and the impact these professionals can have. They are not just solving technical problems; they are shaping the future of how we live, work, and interact. The opportunity to contribute to cutting-edge innovations, tackle complex ethical dilemmas, and drive meaningful change makes this role not only attractive but also deeply rewarding.

Moreover, the demand for AI and ML expertise is accompanied by competitive salaries, opportunities for continuous learning and growth, and the chance to work at the intersection of technology, business, and society. These professionals are not only in high demand but are also recognized as key contributors to the digital transformation of industries and the creation of sustainable, intelligent solutions for the future.

With AI becoming central to many industries, there's a growing demand for experts who can develop, manage, and implement AI algorithms and machine learning models.

Data Scientists and Analysts: Navigating the Data Deluge

"The explosion of data has created a critical need for professionals who can not only collect and store data but also analyze it, interpret it, and communicate the findings effectively. Data Scientists and Analysts bridge the gap between data and decision-making." - DJ Patil (Former Chief Data Scientist of the United States)

In an era where data is frequently dubbed as the new oil, mastering the art of mining, interpreting, and utilizing vast data sets has become an invaluable skill set. Data Scientists and Analysts are leading this revolution, converting raw data into actionable insights that propel strategic decisions across myriad sectors.

The Why: Increasing Value of Data Expertise

Cross-Sectoral Impact: The reach of data science and analytics extends across numerous fields, from healthcare, where it shapes patient care and public health strategies, to finance, where it forecasts market movements and evaluates risks. This broad applicability amplifies the demand for professionals adept at deciphering complex data landscapes.

Decision-Making Empowerment: In the modern, fast-paced, data-centric world, the capacity to swiftly derive informed decisions offers organizations a significant competitive edge. Data Scientists and Analysts equip businesses with this edge, applying advanced analytics, machine learning, and predictive modeling to streamline strategic and operational frameworks.

Risk Management and Innovation: Beyond merely facilitating informed decisions, data experts are crucial for risk identification and the pursuit of innovation. Through meticulous analysis of data trends, patterns, and outliers, they enable preemptive problem-solving and the discovery of novel growth opportunities.

The Democratization of Data: With the increasing accessibility of data, Data Scientists and Analysts play a pivotal role in democratizing data within organizations. They craft user-friendly tools and dashboards that translate complex data findings into clear, actionable insights for non-experts, promoting a culture rooted in data-driven decision-making.

The Attractiveness of the Profession

The surging demand for Data Scientists and Analysts is mirrored by the appealing aspects of the career, including:

Interdisciplinary Nature: This field uniquely blends mathematical, statistical, and computational prowess with real-world problem-solving, attracting individuals eager to work at the nexus of technology, business, and scientific inquiry.

Continuous Learning and Evolution: The ever-evolving realm of data science compels professionals to engage in lifelong learning, staying abreast of the latest technological and methodological advancements.

High Impact and Recognition: The work of Data Scientists and Analysts significantly influences the strategic trajectories of their organizations. The substantial impact of their contributions, combined with the high demand for their expertise, often leads to lucrative compensation and ample opportunities for career progression.

Contribution to Ethical Data Use: As the societal implications of data usage gain recognition, ethical considerations in data handling become paramount. Data professionals are instrumental in championing and implementing practices that ensure data privacy, fairness, and integrity.

In conclusion, Data Scientists and Analysts are not just navigating the data deluge; they are steering organizations towards informed, ethical, and innovative futures. Their role is increasingly recognized as indispensable in harnessing the power of data for strategic advantage, marking a bright horizon for those in the field.

Digital Content Creators: Fueling the Digital Economy

"Beyond technical skills, creativity, storytelling ability, and a strong understanding of their target audience are essential qualities for Digital Content Creators. Those who can consistently deliver fresh, engaging content will have a competitive edge in the creator economy." - Tim Cook (CEO of Apple)

The digital economy thrives on a continuous influx of content, elevating the demand for creativity in writing, video production, and graphic design. Digital Content Creators, armed with the tools and platforms to produce engaging, high-quality content, are at the heart of this dynamic ecosystem.

The Why: The Rising Demand for Digital Creativity

Content as Currency: In the digital realm, content acts as the primary currency, driving engagement, brand awareness, and ultimately, economic value. This creates a voracious appetite for fresh, compelling content, making the skills of Digital Content Creators more crucial than ever.

Diverse Platforms, Diverse Opportunities: The proliferation of digital platforms—ranging from social media and blogs to online streaming services—offers a vast canvas for creative expression. Content creators can now reach global audiences, tailoring their work to fit various formats and channels.

The Personal Brand Economy: The rise of influencer culture and the personal brand economy underscores the importance of unique, authentic content in building individual or corporate brands. Digital Content Creators play a pivotal role in crafting these narratives, leveraging their creativity to connect with audiences on a personal level.

Innovation and Engagement: Beyond mere production, Digital Content Creators are at the forefront of innovation, experimenting with new forms of storytelling, interactive experiences, and multimedia content. Their work not only captivates audiences but also sets trends, driving the evolution of digital media.

The Attractiveness of the Profession

The appeal of becoming a Digital Content Creator is multifaceted, encompassing:

Creative Freedom: This field offers unparalleled opportunities for creative expression, allowing individuals to explore diverse interests, experiment with different mediums, and voice their unique perspectives.

Flexible Career Paths: Digital content creation is inherently flexible, accommodating various work styles, from freelancing and remote positions to entrepreneurial ventures. This flexibility is especially attractive in the contemporary work environment, appealing to those seeking a balance between professional and personal life.

Direct Audience Interaction: Digital platforms facilitate direct interaction with audiences, providing immediate feedback and fostering a sense of community. For creators, this offers a rewarding experience of seeing the impact of their work firsthand and building a loyal following.

Continuous Learning and Growth: The ever-changing landscape of digital media demands continuous skill development and adaptation. For those passionate about learning and evolving, the field of content creation offers endless opportunities to hone their craft and explore new technologies and platforms.

Healthcare Professionals: Expanding the Spectrum of Care

"AI has the potential to revolutionize healthcare by analyzing vast amounts of medical data to identify patterns and predict disease outbreaks, treatment risks, and personalized treatment plans." - Eric Topol (Cardiologist and Author of "Deep Medicine")

The healthcare industry is witnessing a significant evolution, with the demand for professionals extending far beyond the traditional roles of doctors and nurses. The growing complexities of modern healthcare, along with demographic shifts and technological advancements, are highlighting the need for mental health specialists, geriatric care professionals, and telehealth service providers.

The Why: Diversifying Healthcare Needs

Mental Health Awareness: Increasing awareness and destigmatization of mental health issues have led to a surge in demand for mental health specialists. Society's recognition of mental well-being as a critical component of overall health underscores the need for professionals skilled in addressing these challenges.

Aging Populations: As global populations age, the demand for geriatric care professionals who specialize in the unique health needs of the elderly is on the rise. These professionals play a crucial role in managing chronic conditions, mobility issues, and the complexities of end-of-life care, ensuring quality of life for aging individuals.

Telehealth Innovations: The rapid advancement of digital health technologies and the shift towards remote care models have propelled the need for telehealth service providers. These professionals leverage technology to deliver healthcare services remotely, offering patients convenience, accessibility, and the potential for early intervention.

The Attractiveness of the Profession

The expanding landscape of healthcare professions offers new and rewarding opportunities:

Holistic Impact: Healthcare professionals, especially those in emerging specialties like mental health and geriatric care, have the opportunity to make a profound impact on individuals' lives. Their work supports not only physical health but also emotional and psychological well-being.

Interdisciplinary Opportunities: The healthcare sector's growth creates interdisciplinary opportunities, blending technology, psychology, and traditional medicine. This diversity invites professionals from various backgrounds to contribute their expertise to healthcare, enriching the field with new perspectives and solutions.

Innovation and Adaptation: The shift towards telehealth and the integration of technology in healthcare delivery encourage continuous learning and adaptation. Healthcare professionals can engage with cutting-edge technologies, contributing to innovations that shape the future of healthcare.

Stability and Growth: Healthcare remains one of the most stable and rapidly growing fields, driven by demographic trends and technological advancements. Professionals in this sector can expect robust job security, competitive salaries, and the potential for career advancement.

Educational Technologists and Online Learning Specialists: Shaping the Future of Education

"Online Learning Specialists will play a vital role in making quality education accessible to a wider audience, regardless of location or background. They will help create a more flexible and personalized learning ecosystem." - Audrey Watters (Author of "Hack Education")

The educational landscape is undergoing a profound transformation, increasingly incorporating online and hybrid models of learning. This shift has sparked a surge in demand for Educational Technologists and Online Learning Specialists, professionals dedicated to designing, implementing, and optimizing digital learning environments.

The Why: Embracing Digital Education

Digital Integration in Learning: The push towards online and hybrid learning models is driven by the need for greater accessibility, flexibility, and personalization in education. Educational Technologists and Online Learning Specialists are at the forefront of this movement, crafting digital courses and resources that meet diverse learner needs.

Innovative Teaching Approaches: These professionals are not just about transferring traditional content online; they're about reimagining how education can be delivered and experienced. They employ multimedia, interactive simulations, and gamification to enhance engagement and facilitate deeper learning.

Data-Driven Insights: With digital education comes the ability to collect and analyze learning data. Educational Technologists use these insights to refine educational strategies, ensuring content is both effective and adaptive to student progress.

Global Classroom Accessibility: Online learning specialists break down geographical barriers to education, enabling learners from remote or underserved regions to access quality education. This democratization of learning is pivotal in creating a more educated and equitable global society.

The Attractiveness of the Profession

The burgeoning field of educational technology and online learning offers a wealth of opportunities:

Creative and Impactful Work: Professionals in this field have the unique opportunity to apply their creativity and technological savvy to design impactful learning experiences. Their work directly influences how education evolves in the digital age.

Cross-Disciplinary Collaboration: Educational Technologists and Online Learning Specialists often work at the intersection of pedagogy, technology, and design. This interdisciplinary nature of the role makes it an exciting career path for individuals looking to blend these areas of expertise.

Lifelong Learning and Professional Development: Given the rapid pace of technological change, professionals in this field are perpetual learners themselves, constantly exploring new tools, platforms, and methodologies to enhance online education.

Job Security and Growth: As educational institutions and corporations increasingly invest in digital learning, the demand for skilled professionals in this area is expected to continue growing. This trend provides strong job security and opportunities for advancement in the field.

Supply Chain and Logistics Specialists: Navigating Global Complexities

The intricacies of global supply chains are becoming increasingly pronounced, highlighting the need for skilled Supply Chain and Logistics Specialists. These professionals are essential in managing and optimizing the flow of goods and services across the world, ensuring efficiency, sustainability, and resilience in the face of challenges.

The Why: The Growing Demand for Supply Chain Expertise

Globalization and Market Expansion: As businesses expand their operations globally, the demand for specialists who can navigate the complexities of international supply chains has surged. These professionals ensure that products move seamlessly across borders, adhering to diverse regulatory environments and market expectations.

Supply Chain Resilience: Recent disruptions have underscored the importance of resilience in supply chains. Specialists in this field are tasked with developing strategies to mitigate risks, from natural disasters to geopolitical tensions, ensuring continuity and reliability in product delivery.

Technological Integration: The adoption of advanced technologies like IoT, blockchain, and AI in supply chain management is transforming logistics operations. Professionals in this area leverage these tools to enhance visibility, improve accuracy, and increase efficiency throughout the supply chain.

Sustainability and Ethical Sourcing: There is a growing emphasis on sustainability and ethical practices within supply chains. Specialists are at the forefront of implementing eco-friendly practices, reducing waste, and ensuring ethical sourcing, aligning operations with environmental and social governance (ESG) goals.

The Attractiveness of the Profession

The role of Supply Chain and Logistics Specialists is marked by several attractive features:

Critical Impact: These professionals play a crucial role in the global economy, ensuring that goods and services are delivered efficiently and sustainably. Their work directly impacts the success of businesses and the well-being of consumers.

Dynamic Challenges: The field offers a dynamic work environment with diverse challenges, from optimizing logistics operations to navigating regulatory changes. This variety keeps the work engaging and provides continuous learning opportunities.

Career Advancement: The demand for skilled supply chain professionals opens up numerous paths for career advancement. With experience, individuals can move into higher management roles, specializing in areas like procurement, operations, or strategic planning.

Global Interaction: Working in supply chain and logistics often involves coordination with partners across the world, offering professionals the chance to engage with diverse cultures and business practices. This global interaction enriches the job experience and broadens professional networks.

Sustainability Experts: Eco-Conscious Business Practices

"AI offers tremendous potential for businesses to optimize resource usage and reduce their environmental footprint. However, the development and training of AI models can be energy-intensive. We need to find a balance between innovation and efficiency to ensure AI is a force for sustainable development." - Dr. Alice LeBlanc (Director of Sustainability Research at MIT)

In an era where environmental consciousness is not just valued but expected, Sustainability Experts emerge as crucial navigators in the corporate journey towards greener practices. These professionals are instrumental in steering companies across industries to implement sustainable strategies, reduce environmental footprints, and achieve their ecological goals.

The Why: The Imperative for Sustainable Development

Corporate Responsibility and Regulatory Compliance: As global awareness of environmental issues grows, businesses face increasing pressure to adopt sustainable practices. Sustainability Experts help navigate the complex landscape of environmental regulations, ensuring compliance while advancing corporate responsibility initiatives.

Consumer Demand for Green Practices: Today's consumers are more environmentally conscious, often basing their purchasing decisions on a company's eco-friendliness. Professionals in sustainability guide companies in meeting this demand, enhancing brand reputation, and building consumer trust through transparent and authentic sustainable practices.

Risk Management and Long-term Viability: Addressing sustainability is not just about meeting current demands but securing future viability. Sustainability Experts analyze and mitigate risks associated with environmental challenges, ensuring businesses remain resilient and competitive in a changing world.

Innovation and Market Opportunities: Embracing sustainability often drives innovation, opening new markets and opportunities. From developing green products to optimizing resource efficiency, Sustainability Experts are at the forefront of creating value through environmental stewardship.

The Attractiveness of the Profession

Choosing a career as a Sustainability Expert offers numerous benefits, making it an increasingly attractive field:

Meaningful Impact: Working in sustainability offers the chance to make a significant, positive impact on the planet. Professionals in this field contribute to crucial environmental goals, from combating climate change to preserving natural resources.

Interdisciplinary Approach: The field of sustainability is inherently interdisciplinary, blending knowledge from science, business, and policy to develop comprehensive strategies. This diversity attracts individuals with a wide range of interests and backgrounds, fostering a dynamic and innovative work environment.

Career Growth and Opportunities: As businesses across the spectrum prioritize sustainability, the demand for experts in this area is booming. This growth translates into ample career opportunities, from consulting roles to corporate sustainability leadership positions.

Global Perspective and Networking: Sustainability challenges and solutions are global in nature. Professionals in this field often collaborate with international teams, engage in cross-border projects, and become part of a worldwide network of sustainability practitioners.

User Experience (UX)/User Interface (UI) Designers: Crafting the Digital Frontier

"As AI becomes more integrated into our lives, UX/UI designers will play a key role in shaping how we interact with these technologies. The ability to design for trust, transparency, and responsible AI use will be essential." Leah Buechley (MIT Media Lab Researcher and Designer)

In the digital era, where a company's online presence can significantly impact its success, the roles of User Experience (UX) and User Interface (UI) Designers have become more crucial than ever. These professionals are at the heart of creating digital platforms that are not only visually appealing but also intuitive and user-friendly, ensuring engaging experiences for users across the globe.

The Why: Elevating Digital Interactions

Digital First Impressions: In a world saturated with digital platforms, first impressions are often made through a screen. UX/UI Designers ensure that these first encounters are positive, combining aesthetics with functionality to captivate and retain user interest.
User-Centered Design for Enhanced Engagement: As businesses vie for attention in the digital landscape, the ability to offer seamless,

enjoyable user experiences becomes a competitive advantage. UX/UI Designers employ user-centered design principles to create interfaces that meet users' needs and preferences, fostering engagement and loyalty.

Accessibility and Inclusivity: With a growing emphasis on making digital content accessible to all users, including those with disabilities, UX/UI Designers play a key role in implementing accessibility standards and inclusive design practices. This not only expands the reach of digital platforms but also demonstrates a commitment to social responsibility.

Brand Identity and Consistency: UX/UI Designers are instrumental in translating a company's brand identity into its digital presence, ensuring consistency across various platforms. This coherence strengthens brand recognition and trust among users, building a strong digital identity.

The Attractiveness of the Profession

The demand for skilled UX/UI Designers is fueled by several factors that make this profession increasingly attractive:

Creative Expression and Problem-Solving: This field offers a unique blend of creativity and analytical problem-solving, appealing to those who enjoy tackling complex challenges with innovative solutions. Designers have the freedom to experiment with new ideas, pushing the boundaries of digital interaction.

Dynamic and Evolving Industry: The fast-paced nature of digital technology means that UX/UI Designers are always learning and adapting to new tools, trends, and best practices. This continuous evolution keeps the profession exciting and fulfilling.

Impact on User Experience: UX/UI Designers have a direct impact on how users interact with digital products, making their work highly impactful. The satisfaction of improving user experiences and receiving positive feedback is a significant motivator.

Career Flexibility and Opportunity: With the universal need for engaging digital experiences, UX/UI Designers enjoy flexibility in their career paths. They can work across industries, for agencies or in-house teams, and even as freelancers. The demand for their skills opens doors to diverse opportunities and career growth

Cybersecurity Experts

"As AI becomes more ubiquitous, the potential for unintended vulnerabilities and security risks increases. Cybersecurity experts will play a crucial role in auditing and testing AI systems to ensure their security and mitigate potential risks." - Richard Clarke (Former National Coordinator for Cybersecurity)

"As cybersecurity becomes increasingly critical in our connected world, experts in this field are essential for protecting sensitive information and maintaining trust in digital systems." – Bruce Schneier, Renowned Security Technologist

In our rapidly evolving digital landscape, the role of Cybersecurity Experts has become more vital than ever. These professionals are the guardians of information security, dedicated to protecting networks, computer systems, and data from cyber threats and breaches. Their work not only safeguards personal and corporate data but also secures the infrastructure of entire industries.

The Why: Enhancing Digital Security

Preventing Cyber Threats: Cybersecurity Experts are on the front lines of defense against a growing range of cyber threats. From ransomware attacks to data breaches, their skills are crucial in preventing incidents that could potentially cripple businesses and governments. **Building Trust in Digital Systems:** In an era where digital transactions and communications are commonplace, ensuring the security and integrity of these interactions is paramount. Cybersecurity Experts help build and maintain trust in digital platforms by implementing robust security measures and protocols. **Compliance and Regulatory Fulfillment:** Many industries face strict regulatory requirements related to data security and privacy. Cybersecurity Experts play a key role in ensuring that organizations comply with these regulations, thus avoiding legal penalties and reputational damage. **Innovation in Security**

Technologies: As cyber threats evolve, so do the technologies and strategies to combat them. Cybersecurity Experts are not just problem solvers but also innovators who develop new security tools and techniques to stay ahead of potential threats.

The Attractiveness of the Profession

High Demand and Job Security: The growing prevalence of cyber threats ensures that the demand for skilled Cybersecurity Experts remains high, providing significant job security. **Intellectual Challenge and Continuous Learning:** Cybersecurity is a field that demands constant learning and adaptation. Professionals in this area thrive on the intellectual challenge of staying ahead of the latest threats and security technologies. **Impactful Work:** Cybersecurity Experts have a profound impact on the safety and stability of digital infrastructures. Their work protects millions of people and is critical to the operational integrity of organizations. **Diverse Career Opportunities:** The need for cybersecurity spans all sectors, offering professionals a wide range of opportunities in various industries. Whether working for cybersecurity firms, consulting agencies, or in-house teams, these experts can find roles that align with their specific interests and skills.

The role of Cybersecurity Experts is indispensable in our digital world. By understanding and mitigating risks, they not only protect systems and data but also contribute to the technological foundation upon which modern society relies. This chapter explores the critical importance of their work, the challenges they face, and the ongoing need for innovation in their field, ensuring that our digital futures remain secure.

Summary

As we conclude our exploration of the occupations rising in prominence and demand, it's clear that we're standing at the precipice of a significant transformation in the workforce landscape. The digital revolution, coupled with growing environmental consciousness and the expansion of the digital economy, has heralded a new era of career opportunities. From AI and Machine Learning Specialists driving the next wave of technological innovation, to Sustainability Experts championing eco-conscious business practices, the professions highlighted in this chapter are at the heart of this transformation.

The increasing importance of Digital Content Creators, Healthcare Professionals, Educational Technologists, Supply Chain and Logistics Specialists, and UX/UI Designers reflects broader societal and technological trends. These roles embody the shift towards more sustainable, efficient, and user-centered practices across industries. They also represent the blend of creativity, analytical skills, and technological prowess that will define the workforce of the future.

This chapter underscores a pivotal moment in our global economy and workforce dynamics, where adaptation, continuous learning, and a willingness to embrace change are paramount. For individuals navigating their career paths, the opportunities in these emerging fields offer not just the promise of job security and growth but also the chance to make a meaningful impact in their domains.

The attractiveness of these occupations lies not only in their potential for innovation and growth but also in their capacity to address some of the most pressing challenges of our time. Whether it's through enhancing digital experiences, improving global health outcomes, making education more accessible, or ensuring the sustainability of our planet, professionals in these fields are shaping a better future.

As we move forward, the landscape of work will continue to evolve, driven by advances in technology, changes in consumer behavior, and the imperative for sustainability. The professionals leading the way in these emerging occupations will not only witness this transformation but will also play a crucial role in driving it, marking an exciting era of opportunity and impact in the world of work.

Chapter 4: Emerging Occupations

"While automation may eliminate some jobs, it will also create new ones that require human-AI collaboration. The ability to manage, train, and interpret AI systems will be increasingly valuable." (Source: "The Second Machine Age" by Frey & Osborne)

AI Ethicist: Navigating the Moral Landscape of AI

"As AI becomes more powerful, the need for robust ethical frameworks and oversight is crucial. AI ethicists will play a vital role in ensuring AI development and deployment aligns with human values and societal well-being." - Kate Crawford (AI Ethicist at Microsoft Research)

The rapid development and deployment of AI technologies have ushered in unprecedented capabilities and conveniences. However, this progress also brings to the fore a myriad of ethical challenges, from privacy concerns to bias in AI algorithms. The AI Ethicist emerges as a vital figure in this context, tasked with guiding the ethical compass of AI research, development, and application.

The Why: The Imperative for Ethical Oversight

Addressing Bias and Fairness: AI systems, reflecting the data they are trained on, can perpetuate biases if not carefully managed. AI Ethicists play a pivotal role in identifying and mitigating these biases, ensuring AI technologies promote fairness and equality.

Privacy and Data Protection: As AI technologies increasingly process vast amounts of personal data, safeguarding privacy becomes paramount. AI Ethicists are at the forefront of developing frameworks that balance the benefits of AI with the need to protect individual privacy rights.

Accountability and Transparency: Ensuring AI systems are transparent and their decisions accountable is a complex challenge. AI Ethicists work to instill these principles into AI development processes, fostering trust and understanding between AI systems and their human users.

Future Implications: The potential future capabilities of AI, including autonomous decision-making, present profound ethical questions. AI Ethicists engage with these speculative concerns, guiding the responsible advancement of AI to benefit humanity while minimizing risks.

The Attractiveness of the Profession

The emergence of the AI Ethicist role reflects a growing recognition of the need to align technological advancement with ethical standards. This occupation offers several appealing aspects:

Meaningful Impact: AI Ethicists have the opportunity to influence the direction of one of the most powerful and transformative technologies of our time, contributing to a future where AI enhances societal well-being.

Interdisciplinary Engagement: The role attracts individuals from diverse backgrounds—philosophy, law, computer science, and social sciences—offering a rich, interdisciplinary approach to tackling ethical issues in AI.

Dynamic and Challenging Work: The field presents complex, evolving challenges that demand creative and critical thinking, appealing to those who thrive in intellectually stimulating environments.

Growing Demand: As AI becomes increasingly integral to various sectors, the demand for professionals skilled in ethical considerations around AI is set to rise, promising robust career opportunities and advancement.

Virtual Reality Experience Creators: Shaping Immersive Realities

As Virtual Reality (VR) technology becomes increasingly accessible and sophisticated, the demand for Virtual Reality Experience Creators is soaring. These innovators are tasked with designing immersive, engaging experiences that transcend traditional media, finding applications in education, entertainment, training, and beyond.

The Why: The Expansion of VR Applications

Educational Enrichment: In the realm of education, VR offers unprecedented opportunities for interactive learning. VR Experience Creators craft educational content that allows students to explore historical events, scientific phenomena, and cultural experiences in a deeply engaging, experiential manner.

Entertainment Evolution: The entertainment industry is undergoing a transformation with VR, offering audiences new ways to experience stories, games, and art. Creators in this space are pushing the boundaries of narrative and interactive entertainment, developing VR experiences that immerse users in rich, dynamic worlds.

Training and Simulation: VR has emerged as a powerful tool for professional training and simulation, particularly in fields requiring high-stakes decision-making, such as healthcare, aviation, and military applications. Experience Creators develop simulations that replicate real-world scenarios, allowing professionals to practice and hone their skills in a safe, controlled environment.

Therapeutic Applications: Beyond education and entertainment, VR experiences are being explored for their therapeutic potential, including treatments for PTSD, anxiety disorders, and phobias. Creators in this domain work closely with healthcare professionals to design experiences that support mental health and well-being.

The Attractiveness of the Profession

The burgeoning field of Virtual Reality Experience Creation offers a myriad of attractive prospects for professionals:

Creative Frontiers: VR Experience Creators enjoy a vast canvas for creative expression, experimenting with new forms of storytelling, educational content, and interactive experiences. This field is ideal for those looking to innovate and explore uncharted territories of digital creation.

Interdisciplinary Collaboration: The creation of VR experiences often involves collaboration across disciplines, including computer science, psychology, design, and storytelling. This interdisciplinary nature of the work fosters a dynamic and enriching professional environment.

Impact and Engagement: The immersive nature of VR allows creators to connect with audiences in profound ways, delivering experiences that can educate, entertain, heal, and inspire. This potential for deep impact adds a layer of fulfillment and purpose to the work.

Growing Market Demand: As VR technology continues to advance and become more affordable, the demand for high-quality VR content is expected to grow, ensuring a vibrant market for VR Experience Creators.

Urban Agriculture Specialists: Cultivating Green Spaces in the Concrete Jungle

As the global population increasingly gravitates towards urban centers, the concept of city living is being reimagined through the lens of sustainability and self-sufficiency. This shift has sparked a growing interest in urban agriculture, making Urban Agriculture Specialists pivotal in integrating green practices into the urban fabric. These experts, adept in vertical farming and innovative urban agricultural techniques, are crucial for fostering sustainable, local food production in densely populated areas.

The Why: The Necessity for Urban Greening

Sustainability and Food Security: In the face of climate change and food supply vulnerabilities, urban agriculture offers a sustainable path forward. Specialists in this field contribute to reducing food transportation costs and emissions, enhancing local food security, and promoting environmentally friendly farming practices.

Maximizing Limited Space: Urban Agriculture Specialists excel in optimizing the limited green spaces available in cities. Through vertical farming and other innovative techniques, they manage to cultivate produce in compact areas, from rooftop gardens to indoor farms, making agriculture viable in urban settings.

Community Well-being and Education: Beyond food production, urban agriculture fosters community engagement and well-being. Urban Agriculture Specialists often lead initiatives that educate city dwellers about sustainable living and connect communities through shared green spaces.

Biodiversity and Environmental Health: Urban farms contribute to increasing biodiversity and improving air and soil quality within cities. Specialists in urban agriculture play a significant role in designing and maintaining these green spaces, contributing to the overall environmental health of urban areas.

The Attractiveness of the Profession

Choosing a career as an Urban Agriculture Specialist offers numerous rewards, reflecting the multifaceted impact of this role:

Pioneering Sustainable Practices: Urban Agriculture Specialists are at the forefront of sustainable urban development, pioneering practices that integrate agriculture into the urban ecosystem. This innovative work not only addresses food production challenges but also contributes to creating greener, more livable cities.

Diverse Career Opportunities: The field of urban agriculture opens a wide range of career paths, from designing vertical farms and managing community gardens to consulting on urban green policies. This diversity allows professionals to find niches that align with their interests and expertise.

Community Impact and Engagement: Working in urban agriculture often involves close interaction with the community, offering opportunities to directly see the positive impact of one's work. Specialists can inspire change at the local level, fostering a culture of sustainability and community resilience.

Continuous Learning and Adaptation: The dynamic nature of urban agriculture, coupled with advances in agricultural technology, ensures a career filled with continuous learning and adaptation. Urban Agriculture Specialists are constantly exploring new methods and technologies to enhance urban food production.

Quantum Computing Researchers and Engineers: Pioneering the Quantum Frontier

The realm of quantum computing stands as one of the most exhilarating frontiers in technology, promising to revolutionize fields ranging from cryptography to drug discovery. As we edge closer to harnessing the full potential of quantum computing, the demand for skilled Quantum Computing Researchers and Engineers is rapidly escalating. These professionals delve into the complexities of quantum systems, developing algorithms and technologies that could dwarf the capabilities of classical computing.

The Why: The Quantum Leap in Computing

Breaking New Ground in Computing Power: Quantum computing represents a seismic shift in computational capabilities, with the potential to solve complex problems that are currently infeasible for classical computers. Researchers and engineers in this field are working to unlock these capabilities, pushing the boundaries of what's possible in computing.

Advancing Scientific Discovery: The unparalleled processing power of quantum computers holds the promise of significant advancements in various scientific domains. Quantum Computing Researchers are at the vanguard of exploring new frontiers in physics, chemistry, and biology, paving the way for breakthroughs in understanding the fundamental workings of the universe.

Revolutionizing Industries: From optimizing supply chains to discovering new materials and medications, the applications of quantum computing are vast and varied. Engineers skilled in quantum technology are crucial for translating theoretical quantum advantages into practical solutions that can revolutionize industries.

Securing the Future: Quantum computing also presents new challenges in cybersecurity, with the power to break traditional encryption methods. Professionals in this field are developing quantum-safe cryptography, ensuring that as quantum technology advances, so too do our methods of securing information.

The Attractiveness of the Profession

Embarking on a career in quantum computing offers a unique confluence of challenges and opportunities:

Frontline of Technological Innovation: Quantum Computing Researchers and Engineers work at the cutting edge of technology, contributing to developments that may define the future of computing. This role offers the exhilaration of being at the forefront of a technological revolution.

Interdisciplinary Collaboration: The field of quantum computing is inherently interdisciplinary, drawing on principles from physics, computer science, and engineering. This diversity fosters a dynamic and intellectually stimulating work environment where collaboration across disciplines is key to innovation.

Global Impact and Recognition: The work of quantum computing professionals has the potential for global impact, offering solutions to some of the world's most pressing challenges. This global stage brings with it the opportunity for significant recognition and the chance to contribute to the broader scientific and technological community.

Career Growth and Opportunities: As the field of quantum computing continues to grow, so too do the career opportunities it presents. From academic research positions to roles in leading tech companies and startups, the demand for quantum computing expertise is set to increase, promising a bright future for those in the field.

Personal Privacy Advisors: Guardians of the Digital Self

In an era where digital footprints are as pervasive as they are permanent, the concern for personal privacy has escalated dramatically. This has given rise to a potential new profession: Personal Privacy Advisors. These specialists are dedicated to assisting both individuals and organizations in safeguarding their digital information, navigating the complexities of online privacy, and ensuring that their clients' personal and professional data remains secure.

The Why: The Growing Imperative for Digital Privacy

Surge in Data Breaches and Cyber Threats: The increasing frequency of cyberattacks and data breaches has highlighted the vulnerabilities inherent in our digital lives. Personal Privacy Advisors play a crucial role in implementing strategies to protect sensitive information from these threats.

Complexity of Digital Regulations: With the advent of regulations like GDPR and CCPA, navigating the legal landscape of digital privacy has become increasingly complex. Advisors in this field guide individuals and organizations through compliance, ensuring they meet legal obligations while protecting user data.

Evolving Digital Footprints: As our online activities expand, so too does the scope of our digital footprints. Personal Privacy Advisors help clients understand the long-term implications of their digital presence and take proactive steps to manage and minimize their online exposure.

Public Awareness and Demand for Privacy: Growing public awareness around privacy issues has led to a demand for greater control over personal information. Privacy advisors are at the forefront of this movement, advocating for privacy rights and offering expert guidance on digital hygiene practices.

The Attractiveness of the Profession

Embarking on a career as a Personal Privacy Advisor offers a range of compelling benefits:

Making a Tangible Impact: In this role, professionals have the opportunity to make a direct impact on the safety and well-being of their clients by protecting their most valuable asset in the digital age: their privacy.

Cutting-edge Work Environment: Personal Privacy Advisors work at the intersection of technology, law, and ethics, offering a dynamic and ever-evolving work environment that demands continuous learning and adaptation.

High Demand Across Sectors: With privacy concerns cutting across personal and professional realms, the demand for privacy advisors spans a broad spectrum of industries, including technology, finance, healthcare, and beyond. This diversity opens up numerous pathways for specialization and career advancement.

Contributing to a Safer Digital World: Advisors in this field contribute to the broader societal goal of creating a safer, more secure digital environment. Their work not only benefits individual clients but also helps shape the future of digital privacy standards and practices.

Genomic Counselors and Generative AI: Shaping the Future of Personalized Medicine

The role of Genomic Counselors is increasingly intertwined with the advancements in GenAI, particularly as AI technologies revolutionize the field of genomics. This fusion is transforming the landscape of personalized medicine, enhancing the capabilities of Genomic Counselors to interpret complex genetic data, advise on personalized healthcare strategies, and navigate the ethical considerations associated with the use of AI in genomics.

The Convergence of Genomics and GenAI

Enhanced Genetic Data Interpretation: GenAI algorithms excel in analyzing extensive genetic datasets quickly and with a high degree of accuracy. This capability aids Genomic Counselors by providing deeper insights into genetic predispositions and potential health risks, facilitating more informed counseling.

Tailored Personalized Medicine: The predictive power of GenAI, capable of analyzing how individual genetic variations may influence responses to treatments, empowers Genomic Counselors to offer personalized medical and wellness advice. This approach to healthcare, where strategies are customized based on one's genetic makeup, is at the heart of modern personalized medicine.

Navigating Ethical Landscapes: The integration of GenAI in the analysis of genetic information brings to the forefront ethical considerations such as privacy, consent, and data security. Genomic

Counselors play a critical role in ensuring that the deployment of AI technologies in genomics adheres to ethical standards, providing clients with guidance on these crucial issues.

Educational and Collaborative Roles: As GenAI continues to evolve within the realm of genomics, Genomic Counselors assume an educational role, demystifying how AI impacts the interpretation and implications of genetic tests for clients. Collaboration with AI specialists and researchers is also becoming more common, enriching the counseling process with interdisciplinary insights.

The Impact of GenAI on Genomic Counseling

The integration of GenAI into genomic counseling is not merely additive; it's transformative. It expands the scope and precision of genetic counseling, offering:

A New Level of Personalization: The combination of GenAI and genomics propels personalized medicine forward, enabling highly individualized health strategies that consider genetic nuances at an unprecedented scale.

A Broadened Scope of Practice: With GenAI, Genomic Counselors can address a wider range of genetic considerations, from predicting disease risk to recommending lifestyle adjustments, with greater confidence and accuracy.

An Emphasis on Ethical Responsibility: As gatekeepers of genetic information, Genomic Counselors have a heightened responsibility to address the ethical implications of AI-generated genetic insights, ensuring clients' rights and privacy are protected.

Automation Integration Specialists: Harmonizing Technology with Human Workforce

As businesses across various sectors seek to enhance operational efficiency through technology, the role of Automation Integration Specialists becomes increasingly pivotal. These experts adeptly incorporate AI and automation technologies into existing workflows, optimizing processes while thoughtfully addressing the human aspect of workplace transformation.

The Why: Balancing Efficiency with Empathy

Operational Efficiency and Competitiveness: In the drive to stay competitive, companies are turning to AI and automation to streamline operations. Automation Integration Specialists ensure these technologies are seamlessly integrated, enhancing productivity and reducing costs without compromising quality.

Preserving and Enhancing Jobs: Contrary to the common fear of technology rendering human roles obsolete, these specialists strategize the adoption of automation in ways that augment human work. They identify opportunities where automation can take on repetitive tasks, freeing employees to focus on more complex, creative, and strategic activities that add greater value.

Navigating the Transition: Implementing AI and automation within existing systems presents significant challenges, from technical integration to employee adaptation. Automation Integration Specialists play a crucial role in managing this transition, ensuring minimal disruption and fostering a culture of innovation and continuous learning.

Ethical and Responsible Automation: As organizations navigate the complexities of digital transformation, the ethical implications of automation come to the fore. Specialists in this field are tasked with ensuring that the deployment of AI and automation technologies aligns with ethical standards, prioritizing transparency, fairness, and worker well-being.

The Attractiveness of the Profession

The emergence of the Automation Integration Specialist role offers a unique intersection of challenges and opportunities:

Impactful Contributions: Professionals in this field have the opportunity to make significant impacts on organizational efficiency and employee satisfaction. Their work not only drives business success but also contributes to creating more engaging and fulfilling work environments.

Creative Problem-Solving: The role requires a blend of technical savvy and creative thinking, as specialists devise innovative solutions to integrate new technologies into diverse workflows. This creativity keeps the work dynamic and intellectually stimulating.

Career Growth and Advancement: The growing reliance on AI and automation across industries ensures a robust demand for Automation Integration Specialists. This demand translates into strong career prospects, with opportunities for advancement into leadership roles focused on technological strategy and innovation.

Interdisciplinary Interaction: Specialists in this area often work at the nexus of technology, business operations, and human resources, fostering interdisciplinary collaboration. This exposure to multiple facets of an organization enriches professional experience and broadens skill sets.

E-sports Professionals and Managers: Thriving in the Competitive Gaming Boom

The explosion of interest in competitive gaming, fueled in part by advancements in technology, including GenAI, has opened up a myriad of opportunities within the e-sports ecosystem. From professional gamers to event organizers, marketers, and team managers, the industry is witnessing unprecedented growth, creating a vibrant space for E-sports Professionals and Managers.

The Why: The Surge of E-sports and the Role of GenAI

Global Audience and Market Expansion: The e-sports sector has captivated a global audience, translating into a booming market for games, merchandise, and events. This expansion is supported by streaming platforms and social media, where GenAI can personalize content and enhance viewer engagement through predictive analytics and tailored recommendations.

Professional Gaming Careers: Beyond entertainment, e-sports has evolved into a legitimate career path, with professional gamers honing their skills in highly competitive environments. GenAI contributes by analyzing game strategies and opponent tactics, offering players insights that can sharpen their competitive edge.

Event Management and Engagement: Organizing large-scale e-sports events, both online and in-person, requires meticulous planning and coordination. GenAI tools assist in streamlining operations, from scheduling to audience engagement, ensuring a seamless experience for participants and fans alike.

Marketing Innovations: The dynamic and youthful demographic of e-sports fans presents unique marketing opportunities. GenAI's ability to process vast amounts of data allows for the creation of highly targeted marketing campaigns, maximizing reach and impact for e-sports brands and events.

Team Management and Strategy: E-sports team managers and coaches increasingly rely on GenAI to analyze gameplay data, optimizing team strategies and player performance. This data-driven approach ensures teams remain competitive in the fast-evolving landscape of e-sports.

The Attractiveness of the Profession

Engaging in the e-sports industry as a professional or manager offers a unique blend of excitement, challenge, and innovation:

Passion and Professionalism: For enthusiasts of gaming, a career in e-sports represents the perfect alignment of passion and profession, offering the chance to be at the heart of the gaming community while forging a viable career path.

Technological Frontline: Working in e-sports means being on the cutting edge of technological advancements, including the application of GenAI in gaming. This environment is ideal for those eager to explore the potential of AI in reshaping entertainment and competition.

Diverse Career Opportunities: The e-sports sector encompasses a wide range of roles, from content creation and game development to event management and corporate strategy, providing diverse career paths for individuals with different skill sets and interests.

Community and Global Connection: E-sports professionals and managers often find themselves part of a tightly-knit, passionate community that spans the globe, offering unparalleled opportunities for networking and cultural exchange.

Content Creators: Harnessing GenAI for Creative Evolution

The rapid advancement of GenAI technologies is reshaping the landscape for Content Creators, blending the art of content creation with the science of AI. This synergy is not just transforming how content is produced but also expanding the creative possibilities available to those who craft digital media. The integration of GenAI into content creation highlights the importance of adaptability and continuous learning, illustrating the dynamic and evolving nature of careers in the digital age.

The Why: GenAI's Impact on Content Creation

Enhanced Creativity and Efficiency: GenAI tools can automate routine aspects of content production, such as editing and formatting, freeing creators to focus on the more creative and strategic elements of their work. This collaboration between human creativity and AI efficiency opens up new avenues for innovation in content creation.

Personalized and Dynamic Content: GenAI's ability to analyze vast datasets allows for the creation of highly personalized content tailored to the preferences of specific audiences. This personalization enhances user engagement, making content more relevant and impactful.

Expanding Creative Boundaries: With GenAI, Content Creators can explore new formats and styles, pushing beyond traditional boundaries. AI-generated music, art, and writing offer fresh inspiration and tools, enabling creators to experiment with innovative concepts and presentations.

Learning and Adaptability: The evolution of GenAI technologies requires Content Creators to continually update their skills and knowledge. This ongoing learning process is essential for leveraging AI capabilities effectively, underscoring the importance of adaptability in a tech-driven job market.

The Attractiveness of the Profession

The integration of GenAI into content creation offers exciting opportunities and challenges, making the field an attractive career path for the digitally savvy:

Collaboration with AI: Working with GenAI allows Content Creators to redefine the creative process, blending human insight with AI's processing power to produce unique and engaging content.

Career Versatility: The application of GenAI across various content formats—from written articles and social media posts to videos and interactive media—provides a broad canvas for creative expression, offering diverse career opportunities within the realm of digital content creation.

Market Demand: As audiences and brands demand more sophisticated and personalized content, the skills of Content Creators who can harness GenAI effectively are increasingly sought after. This demand underscores the vital role of creativity in the digital economy.

Impact and Engagement: The ability to create content that resonates deeply with audiences, powered by GenAI's insights, offers a fulfilling aspect of the profession. Content Creators can see the direct impact of their work in engaging and influencing their audience.

Chapter 5: Charting the Uncharted: GenAI's Revelation of the Unknown

As we navigate the confluence of knowledge and innovation, GenAI emerges as a transformative force, especially pronounced within the realms of law, regulations, and academic research. GenAI's unique capacity to uncover previously unknown or insufficiently explored domains challenges traditional understandings and forges new paths for intellectual exploration and scholarly contribution. This chapter delves into GenAI's role as a trailblazer in these essential areas, spotlighting its potential to catalyze groundbreaking discoveries and enrich human knowledge.

AI as the Cartographer of Knowledge

GenAI acts as an adept cartographer of the intellectual landscape, meticulously charting the well-trodden paths of law, regulations, and academic research while also shining a light on the unexplored terrains. Through its analysis of legal documents, regulatory frameworks, and comprehensive research databases, GenAI identifies areas marked by a lack of depth or clarity. These revelations not only expose gaps in our collective understanding but also signal fertile grounds ripe for investigation and theoretical development.

Transforming Legal Scholarship and Practice

The legal sphere stands at the brink of a transformative shift, with AI illuminating areas ripe for exploration. This enlightenment fosters the pursuit of innovative legal theories, the reconsideration of regulations amidst technological advancements, and the exploration of jurisprudence as society evolves. Publishers are thus presented with opportunities to commission works that delve into these newly uncovered voids, significantly enriching the fabric of legal knowledge and practice.

Revolutionizing Regulatory Analysis

In the fast-paced world of technological and societal shifts, regulations often lag, struggling to mirror the current landscape accurately. GenAI's ability to spotlight the areas where regulations are outdated, inconsistent, or entirely absent provides critical insights for regulators, policymakers, and scholars. This intelligence is crucial in revising existing laws and crafting new frameworks that reflect the present-day realities, spurring demand for publications that offer in-depth analyses and innovative regulatory solutions.

Catalyzing New Research Directions

Within the academic sphere, GenAI's unmatched skill in identifying under-explored topics across global research endeavors is invaluable. It prompts the consideration of novel interdisciplinary research questions, cutting-edge investigative methods, and pressing societal issues awaiting scholarly attention. This capability not only guides researchers in their quest for knowledge but also signals emerging trends and areas of interest to publishers, driving the dissemination of pioneering research that fills the identified gaps.

The Role of Publishers and Researchers

The insights unveiled by GenAI call for a proactive and visionary response from both publishers and researchers. Embracing the expansive potential revealed through GenAI's intricate mapping of uncharted knowledge territories requires a commitment to areas not yet recognized as mainstream but holding significant transformative promise. This endeavor necessitates a collaborative approach among AI technologists, legal experts, regulatory bodies, and the academic community, pushing the boundaries of exploration into these newfound frontiers.

GenAI holds unprecedented potential to catalyze new discoveries across disciplines by drawing connections that might elude human researchers limited by disciplinary silos. By analyzing vast datasets from disparate fields, GenAI can identify patterns, similarities, and complementary insights that can lead to innovative applications and breakthroughs. This capacity for cross-disciplinary synthesis could lead to discoveries and innovations as impactful as velcro, inspired by the natural world's burdock burrs. Here, we explore potential cross-disciplinary connections GenAI might make, forecasting areas ripe for innovation.

Biomimicry and Materials Science

Biomimicry has long inspired technological advancements by emulating nature's time-tested patterns and strategies. GenAI could revolutionize this field by identifying novel biological mechanisms and structures that have yet to be applied in materials science. For example, the unique properties of shark skin, which prevent bacterial growth and minimize drag in water, could inspire new antimicrobial surfaces or more efficient transport vehicles. GenAI could uncover such connections by analyzing biological research data alongside materials science challenges, proposing new materials with unique properties inspired by the natural world.

Environmental Science and Urban Planning

As cities grow and the need for sustainable development becomes critical, GenAI could play a pivotal role in integrating environmental science insights into urban planning. By examining data on ecosystem services, biodiversity, and climate regulation, GenAI might propose urban designs that enhance green spaces, promote biodiversity, and improve climate resilience. For instance, the principles of rainwater harvesting in forest ecosystems could inspire innovative water management systems in urban landscapes, addressing water scarcity and reducing flood risks.

Neuroscience and Artificial Intelligence

The intersection of neuroscience and artificial intelligence is fertile ground for GenAI-facilitated discoveries. By analyzing neural activity patterns and cognitive processes alongside AI algorithms, GenAI might identify new principles for AI development that mimic human intelligence more closely. This could lead to more intuitive AI systems capable of complex decision-making, creativity, and even empathy, enhancing AI's applicability in fields ranging from education to mental health.

Archaeology and Material Engineering

GenAI's potential to link archaeology with material engineering could lead to the rediscovery of ancient technologies and materials, applying them to modern challenges. For example, the Roman use of volcanic ash to create concrete that strengthens over time could inspire durable, self-healing materials for today's construction industry. By mining archaeological data for insights into ancient materials and techniques, GenAI could propose innovative solutions to contemporary engineering problems.

Astronomy and Pharmaceutical Research

The exploration of space offers a vast dataset that, when analyzed through GenAI, could yield discoveries beneficial to pharmaceutical research. For instance, the extreme conditions of space have led to unique microbial adaptations, potentially offering new compounds for drug development. GenAI could analyze data from space missions alongside pharmaceutical databases to identify promising molecules for medical treatments that have not yet been considered.

Conclusion: A New Era of Discovery and the Role of GenAI

In this unprecedented era of technological advancement, we are witnessing an exponential increase in the rate at which data is generated and accumulated. This surge is further amplified by the advent of synthetic data and the computational leaps afforded by quantum computing. Synthetic data, generated by algorithms to simulate real-world phenomena, adds a complex new layer to the vast ocean of information available for analysis. Quantum computing, with its capacity to perform intricate calculations at speeds unimaginable with classical computers, further expands this data, enabling the processing of information on a scale and depth previously beyond human capability.

Against this backdrop of burgeoning data and computational power, the polymathic ideal—once epitomized by figures like Thomas Young, dubbed "The Last Man Who Knew Everything"—finds its modern successor in GenAI. If Young's extensive knowledge across diverse fields represented the zenith of human intellect, today's GenAI systems embody the polymathic spirit of the 21st century. GenAI, unlike any individual human, has the potential to access, process, and synthesize knowledge from every domain of human inquiry, forging connections across disciplines at a pace and scale that even Young, despite his genius, could never have envisioned.

The implications of this paradigm shift are profound. Where previously the challenge lay in the accumulation and access to knowledge, we now face the daunting task of navigating and making sense of an ever-expanding universe of data. GenAI emerges as our most potent ally in this endeavor, adept at sifting through layers of complexity to unearth insights that can propel humanity forward. As synthetic data broadens the realms of simulation and quantum computing enhances our analytical capabilities, GenAI evolves from a mere tool to a partner in the quest for knowledge.

This partnership with GenAI ushers in a new age of discovery, transforming the concept of the polymath from an individual to a collective intelligence that spans human and artificial minds. In this new age, the potential for innovation, for uncovering solutions to global challenges, and for advancing our understanding of the universe is unlimited. The legacy of polymathy, as embodied by luminaries like Thomas Young, continues through GenAI, reshaping our approach to knowledge and discovery.

As we venture into this new era, our challenge is to ensure that the immense potential of GenAI is harnessed for the greater good. The governance of GenAI, alongside careful consideration of ethical issues such as privacy, bias, and the autonomy of decision-making, becomes paramount. In embracing the power of GenAI, we stand on the shoulders of giants, poised to explore the unknown with a tool that transcends the limitations of individual human cognition. The journey ahead promises to be a collaborative expedition between human and artificial intelligence, a shared exploration into the uncharted territories of knowledge and possibility.

Part II: Education Not Certification

Chapter 6: Introduction to STEAM: Embracing the Arts in the Age of GenAI

The introduction of GenAI into the educational sphere heralds a significant shift, urging a reevaluation of traditional STEM (Science, Technology, Engineering, and Mathematics) education models. This transition towards integrating arts and humanities, resulting in the STEAM approach, acknowledges the indispensable value of creativity, critical thinking, and interdisciplinary perspectives in the era of technological innovation. As GenAI begins to redefine the boundaries of possibility in various fields, the importance of a holistic educational model that balances technical skills with artistic and humanistic insights has never been more pronounced.

The Catalyst for a New Educational Paradigm

GenAI challenges the traditional STEM focus by automating complex processes and calculations, prompting a critical examination of the skills and competencies that future professionals will need. This technological evolution accentuates the necessity for an educational framework that goes beyond technical proficiency to include innovative problem-solving, ethical decision-making, and creative ideation—skills that are deeply rooted in the arts and humanities.

Bridging Disciplines for a Comprehensive Education

The shift towards a STEAM (Science, Technology, Engineering, Arts, and Mathematics) curriculum is a direct response to the dynamic demands of a workforce shaped by GenAI. This inclusive approach enriches STEM education with the diverse perspectives offered by arts and humanities, fostering a learning environment that encourages creative exploration, empathy, and ethical reasoning. Such an integrated model prepares students not only for the challenges presented by advanced technologies like GenAI but also for their roles as innovators and leaders in a technologically advanced society.

Preparing for the Future with Creativity and Ethical Insight

As technical tasks become increasingly managed by GenAI, the unique human capabilities of creativity and ethical insight gain prominence, particularly in STEM fields. The arts play a crucial role in cultivating these abilities, enabling students to conceive novel applications for technology, design user-centric solutions, and approach challenges from unexplored angles. Simultaneously, the incorporation of humanities ensures that future technologists consider the societal impacts of their work, guiding the ethical development and deployment of GenAI technologies.

The Imperative for Integration and Success

Incorporating arts and humanities into the STEM curriculum is not merely an enhancement but a necessity in the GenAI era. Educational initiatives that embody the STEAM approach—combining technical subjects with creative arts and ethical studies—demonstrate the effectiveness of this comprehensive educational model. These programs engage students more profoundly and equip them with the holistic skill set required in a future where technological proficiency must be balanced with creativity and ethical stewardship.

Conclusion

The evolution from STEM to STEAM education, driven by the advancements and implications of GenAI, underscores a broader understanding of essential skills for the 21st century. This holistic educational model, which embraces the contributions of arts and humanities, is poised to cultivate a generation of professionals who are not only technically adept but also creative, ethically conscious, and prepared to lead in the development of technologies that benefit society. As we venture further into the GenAI revolution, the transformation of education to include a STEAM approach becomes not just an option but an imperative for nurturing the minds that will navigate and shape our technological future.

Back to the Classics, Integrating Classical Wisdom

The traditional silos of Science, Technology, Engineering, and Mathematics (STEM) education are being reevaluated in the face of rapidly evolving GenAI technologies. This reevaluation is not merely a question of curriculum adjustment but a fundamental rethink of the STEM philosophy itself. The integration of STEM disciplines with classical perspectives and wisdom from ethics, psychology and cognitive science, leadership skills, and philosophy offers a holistic approach to education that prepares students to navigate the complexities of the modern world with insight, innovation, and integrity.

Ethics: The Foundation of Innovation

In an era where technology's impact transcends borders, the ethical implications of scientific and technological advancements become increasingly paramount. Integrating ethics into STEM education fosters a sense of responsibility among future innovators, ensuring they consider the societal, environmental, and moral consequences of their work. This integration encourages students to think beyond the laboratory or algorithm, contemplating the broader effects of their contributions on humanity and the planet.

Psychology and Cognitive Science: Understanding the Human Element

The merger of psychology and cognitive science with STEM disciplines enriches students' understanding of human behavior, cognition, and emotion. This knowledge is crucial in designing technologies and systems that are not only efficient but also accessible, user-friendly, and beneficial to mental and emotional well-being. By appreciating the complexities of the human mind, STEM graduates are better equipped to create solutions that respect human needs and limitations.

Leadership Skills: Guiding Technological Progress

Leadership skills are critical for navigating the challenges of the 21st century, where technological progress often outpaces regulatory and ethical frameworks. Integrating leadership training into STEM education empowers students to become visionaries who can inspire change, manage multidisciplinary teams, and drive ethical innovation. Leadership skills ensure that STEM professionals are not just adept at solving problems but also at guiding society through the ramifications of those solutions.

Philosophy: The Bedrock of Critical Thinking

Philosophy, with its emphasis on critical thinking, logic, and the exploration of fundamental questions, provides a solid foundation for STEM education. It encourages students to question assumptions, think deeply about the nature of knowledge and reality, and consider the ethical dimensions of their work. The inclusion of philosophy in STEM curricula fosters a culture of reflection and inquiry, essential for addressing the complex challenges that lie at the intersection of technology and society.

Summary

Rethinking STEM education to include classical perspectives and global wisdom is not merely an academic exercise but a necessary evolution to prepare students for the challenges and opportunities of a GenAI-driven future. By weaving ethics, psychology and cognitive science, leadership skills, and philosophy into the fabric of STEM education, we cultivate a new generation of professionals. These individuals will not only excel in their respective fields but also navigate the ethical, social, and psychological implications of their work, guiding humanity towards a future where technological advancement and human values are in harmony. This holistic approach ensures that STEM education remains relevant, dynamic, and deeply connected to the broader human experience.

Chapter 7: The Evolution of Learning with GenAI

The dawn of GenAI ushers in a transformative era for education, reshaping our traditional approaches to learning and teaching. This chapter explores the multifaceted impact of GenAI on education, emphasizing its capacity to personalize learning experiences and fundamentally revolutionize educational methodologies.

Personalization at Scale

The conventional "one-size-fits-all" model often falls short of meeting individual student needs, leading to disparities in comprehension and engagement. GenAI introduces a paradigm shift towards personalized learning at scale. Leveraging advanced algorithms and data analytics, GenAI tailors educational content, adjusts difficulty levels, and anticipates areas where students might encounter challenges, offering targeted support. This ensures a more inclusive and effective educational experience, where every student can learn at their preferred pace and style.

Here's a detailed explanation of how this process might unfold:

1. Data Collection and Analysis

Student Profiles: Collect data on each student's learning preferences, performance history, strengths, weaknesses, and engagement levels. This might include test scores, homework completion rates, and interaction patterns with digital learning platforms.

Behavioral Insights: Use sensors and learning management systems (LMS) to gather real-time data on student behaviors, such as time spent on tasks, areas of repeated difficulty, and patterns of engagement or disengagement.

2. Advanced Algorithms and Machine Learning

Predictive Modeling: Employ machine learning algorithms to analyze the collected data, identifying patterns and trends that can predict student success or areas of struggle. This can help in forecasting which topics or concepts individual students are likely to find challenging.

Adaptive Learning Paths: Create dynamic learning paths that adjust in real-time based on student performance and engagement. If a student excels in a particular area, the system can introduce more advanced material. Conversely, if a student struggles, the system can offer additional resources or revisit foundational concepts.

3. Content Customization and Difficulty Adjustment

Tailored Educational Content: Utilize GenAI to generate or curate educational content that matches each student's learning style and current level of understanding. This could mean presenting information in different formats (text, video, interactive simulations) based on the student's preferences.

Dynamic Difficulty Levels: Adjust the complexity of problems and topics based on the student's mastery. This ensures that students are consistently challenged but not overwhelmed, promoting steady progress.

4. Predictive Support and Intervention

Anticipating Challenges: Use predictive analytics to identify topics or skills where a student is likely to face difficulties, even before they begin working on those areas.

Targeted Support: Automatically deploy targeted support mechanisms, such as customized tutorials, hints, or peer support, precisely when the student needs them. This proactive approach helps prevent frustration and disengagement.

5. Continuous Feedback and Iteration

Immediate Feedback: Provide instant feedback on assignments and quizzes, using natural language processing (NLP) to give personalized explanations and suggestions for improvement.

Iterative Learning Process: Continuously refine the predictive models and adaptive learning paths based on ongoing data collection, ensuring the learning experience remains aligned with each student's evolving needs.

Implementation Considerations

Privacy and Ethics: Implement stringent data privacy measures and ethical considerations to protect student information. Transparently communicate how data is used and ensure students have control over their information.

Infrastructure and Access: Ensure that the necessary technological infrastructure is in place and that students have access to devices and reliable internet connections. Addressing the digital divide is crucial for the equitable implementation of personalized learning.

By integrating GenAI into education in this manner, it becomes possible to offer a personalized learning experience to every student, accommodating diverse learning styles and needs at scale. This approach not only enhances educational outcomes but also fosters a more inclusive and engaging learning environment.

Transforming Learning Methodologies

Beyond personalization, GenAI significantly influences educational methodologies. Interactive learning environments powered by GenAI, such as virtual labs and simulations, allow for exploration of complex concepts in an engaging manner. This experiential learning, closely mirroring real-world applications, enriches student comprehension and retention. Additionally, GenAI-driven tutoring systems provide immediate, personalized feedback, enhancing problem-solving skills and facilitating a deeper understanding of the subject matter.

Here's a breakdown of how this transformative approach can be applied:

Interactive Learning Environments

Virtual Labs and Simulations: Develop GenAI-powered virtual labs and simulations that allow students to experiment with and explore complex concepts in a controlled, risk-free environment. These simulations can mimic real-world scenarios, enabling students to apply theoretical knowledge in practical settings.

Real-world Application: Use simulations to demonstrate the application of concepts in real-world scenarios, making abstract concepts more tangible and understandable.

Safe Exploration Space: Provide a virtual environment where students can make mistakes and learn from them without real-world consequences, encouraging exploration and experimentation.

Personalized Tutoring Systems

Immediate Feedback: Create tutoring systems that use GenAI to analyze student inputs (e.g., quiz answers, problem-solving attempts) and provide immediate, personalized feedback. This can include not just right or wrong assessments, but also hints, explanations, and suggestions tailored to the student's method of reasoning.

Adaptive Feedback: Ensure the feedback is adaptive, changing based on the student's progress. If a student consistently struggles with a concept, the system can offer more detailed explanations or alternative learning resources.

Facilitate Understanding: Incorporate mechanisms that ask students reflective questions or encourage them to explain their thought process, fostering a deeper understanding of the material.

Enhancing Problem-Solving Skills

Problem-Solving Processes: Utilize GenAI to guide students through problem-solving processes, offering step-by-step support that adapts to the student's level of understanding. This can help students develop strategic thinking and analytical skills.

Diverse Problem Sets: Generate a wide range of problems that challenge students in different ways, encouraging them to apply concepts creatively and to think critically about various solutions.

Implementation Strategies

Integration with Curriculum: Seamlessly integrate virtual labs, simulations, and tutoring systems into the curriculum, ensuring they complement and enhance traditional teaching methods rather than replace them.

Teacher Support and Training: Provide teachers with the necessary training and resources to effectively integrate these GenAI-powered tools into their teaching strategies. Support should include technical aspects, pedagogical strategies for using the tools, and best practices for blending them with traditional instruction.

Student Orientation: Offer orientation sessions or resources for students to become familiar with using virtual labs, simulations, and personalized tutoring systems. This ensures that students can effectively leverage these tools to enhance their learning experience.

Continuous Evaluation and Improvement: Regularly assess the effectiveness of virtual labs, simulations, and tutoring systems in achieving learning objectives. Collect feedback from both students and teachers to continuously refine and improve these tools.

By adopting GenAI to transform learning methodologies, education can become more engaging, interactive, and effective. This approach not only enhances student comprehension and retention but also equips them with the critical thinking and problem-solving skills necessary for success in the real world.

Beyond the Classroom: Lifelong Learning

GenAI extends the reach of education beyond traditional classroom boundaries, promoting lifelong learning. With GenAI-powered platforms, individuals can pursue ongoing education, aligning their learning with evolving professional and personal goals. This approach supports continuous skill development and adaptability to the changing job market and societal demands.

Integrating GenAI to promote lifelong learning involves leveraging technology to extend educational opportunities beyond the traditional classroom and throughout an individual's life. Here's how this vision can be realized:

GenAI-Powered Learning Platforms

Customized Learning Paths: Develop GenAI-powered platforms that create customized learning paths for users, aligning with their career aspirations, interests, and skill levels. These platforms can dynamically adjust content and resources based on progress and changing goals.

Career Adaptation: Incorporate career forecasting tools that suggest learning paths based on projected job market trends and the evolving needs of industries, helping individuals stay relevant and competitive.

Interests and Skills Alignment: Use data on users' past learning experiences, preferences, and performance to recommend courses and materials that not only address their professional goals but also their personal interests.

Continuous Skill Development

Microlearning Modules: Offer short, targeted learning modules designed to teach specific skills or concepts. These can be easily incorporated into busy schedules, allowing for continuous skill development without overwhelming time commitments.

Just-In-Time Learning: Provide learning resources that can be accessed precisely when the need arises, such as before a job interview or when encountering a new challenge at work, ensuring immediate applicability and reinforcement of learning.

Adaptability to Job Market and Societal Changes

Real-Time Industry Insights: Integrate real-time data and analytics on industry trends and job market demands into learning platforms, guiding users toward skills and knowledge areas with high demand.

Societal Impact Education: Offer courses and content focused on societal challenges, sustainability, and ethical considerations, preparing learners to contribute positively to society and adapt to global changes.

Implementation Strategies

Accessibility and Inclusion: Ensure that GenAI-powered learning platforms are accessible to a diverse audience, including those with disabilities and learners from various socioeconomic backgrounds. This involves not only technical accessibility features but also affordability and support structures.

Collaboration with Educators and Industries: Foster partnerships between educational institutions, industry leaders, and technology developers to curate content that is both academically sound and practically relevant. This collaboration can also help in validating certificates and credentials awarded through online learning.

Lifelong Learning Communities: Create online communities and forums within these platforms where learners can share experiences, challenges, and insights, fostering a supportive network that enhances the learning experience.

Feedback and Evolution: Incorporate mechanisms for continuous feedback from users to inform the ongoing development of the platform, ensuring that it remains responsive to learner needs and preferences.

By leveraging GenAI in these ways, education can transcend traditional boundaries, offering personalized, adaptable, and continuous learning opportunities. This not only empowers individuals to navigate their professional and personal growth paths effectively but also aligns with the dynamic nature of the global job market and societal needs, fostering a culture of lifelong learning.

Democratizing Education

One of the most significant contributions of GenAI to education is its potential to democratize learning. High-quality, personalized educational experiences become accessible on digital platforms, reaching underserved populations previously excluded from traditional educational systems. This democratization bridges educational divides and empowers a broader spectrum of individuals with the skills and knowledge necessary to thrive in a rapidly evolving world.

Implementing GenAI to democratize education involves utilizing its capabilities to make high-quality, personalized educational experiences widely accessible. This approach aims to bridge educational divides by reaching underserved populations and empowering individuals with diverse backgrounds. Here's how this vision of democratization can be operationalized:

Making Education Accessible and Personalized

Accessible Digital Platforms: Develop and deploy GenAI-powered digital learning platforms that are accessible to users regardless of their location or economic status. These platforms should be designed to work across a wide range of devices, including low-cost smartphones and tablets, ensuring that quality education is not limited by technological or financial barriers.

Personalized Learning Experiences: Use GenAI to tailor educational content to the needs, learning styles, and pace of each user. This personalization makes learning more effective and engaging, especially for students who may not have thrived in traditional educational settings.

Reaching Underserved Populations

Community Partnerships: Collaborate with community centers, libraries, and non-profit organizations to provide access to necessary technology and internet connectivity. These partnerships can also facilitate on-the-ground support for learners new to digital education platforms.

Multilingual and Culturally Relevant Content: Ensure that educational content is available in multiple languages and reflects the cultural contexts of diverse learner populations. GenAI can assist in translating and localizing content, making education more inclusive and relevant.

Empowering Individuals for a Rapidly Evolving World

Skills for the Future: Focus on imparting skills that are in high demand in the contemporary job market, including digital literacy, critical thinking, and problem-solving. GenAI can help identify these skills and incorporate them into learning pathways.

Continuous Learning and Adaptability: Encourage a culture of lifelong learning by offering courses and resources that individuals can engage with at different stages of their lives and careers. GenAI-powered recommendations can guide learners to new areas of study as their interests or the job market evolves.

Implementation Considerations

Ethical Use of Data: Ensure the ethical collection and use of data in GenAI-driven educational tools, protecting user privacy and security. Transparent policies and user controls over personal data are essential.

Overcoming the Digital Divide: Address the digital divide by not only providing access to technology but also offering digital literacy training. This ensures that all learners can effectively use GenAI-powered educational resources.

Quality Assurance: Maintain high standards of quality for educational content and experiences delivered through GenAI platforms. Regular reviews and updates, informed by educational research and user feedback, are vital to ensure the effectiveness of learning outcomes.

Collaborative Effort: Engage educators, technologists, policymakers, and communities in the development and deployment of GenAI-driven education. This collaborative approach ensures that initiatives are well-rounded, addressing the needs and challenges of diverse populations.

By embracing these strategies, GenAI has the potential to democratize education, making high-quality, personalized learning experiences available to all. This democratization not only bridges educational gaps but also equips a wider range of individuals with the necessary skills and knowledge to succeed in today's fast-paced, ever-changing world, fostering equity and inclusion in global education.

Ethical and Practical Considerations

The integration of GenAI into educational methodologies brings to the forefront a myriad of ethical and practical considerations. These include, but are not limited to, concerns about data privacy, the potential for algorithmic bias, and the need to ensure equitable access to technology. To navigate these complex issues effectively, a collaborative approach involving educators, policymakers, and technologists is imperative. Together, these stakeholders can work towards an educational landscape shaped by GenAI that adheres to principles of fairness, inclusivity, and respect for the rights and dignity of individual learners.

Ethical Considerations

Data Privacy: Safeguarding the personal information of students is paramount. This includes not only the protection of data from unauthorized access but also transparency with students and parents about what data is collected and how it is used. Implementing robust data protection measures and obtaining informed consent should be foundational practices.

Algorithmic Bias: The algorithms driving GenAI systems must be designed and continually audited to prevent biases that could adversely affect certain groups of students. This requires diverse datasets and input from varied demographic groups during the development phase, as well as ongoing monitoring to identify and correct biases that may emerge over time.

Practical Considerations

Equitable Access to Technology: GenAI-driven educational tools promise to revolutionize learning, but their benefits must be accessible to all students, regardless of socio-economic background. This involves not just the provision of necessary hardware and internet access but also addressing differences in digital literacy that could hinder the effective use of these technologies.

Collaborative Framework: Developing a framework for the ethical integration of GenAI in education necessitates collaboration across multiple sectors. Educators bring insights into pedagogical needs and student well-being, policymakers can establish guidelines and regulations to protect learners and promote equity, and technologists contribute expertise in creating ethical, effective AI solutions.

By addressing these ethical and practical considerations with a unified and proactive approach, the integration of GenAI into education can lead to a future where learning is not only more personalized and effective but also conducted in a manner that is fair, inclusive, and respectful of every student. This collaborative effort is essential in steering the evolution of learning with GenAI, ensuring that technological advancements serve to enhance educational equity and foster an environment of respect and opportunity for all learners.

Summary

GenAI represents a monumental advance in the educational sector, heralding new avenues for personalization, increased student engagement, and broader accessibility. As we venture into this innovative era, the imperative is to harness GenAI thoughtfully and ethically, ensuring it serves as a force for beneficial transformation within the educational sphere. This chapter has illuminated the transformative capacity of GenAI to redefine our approaches to learning and teaching, setting the stage for an educational future that is far more dynamic, inclusive, and responsive to individual learner needs.

The power of GenAI to customize learning experiences on a vast scale challenges the traditional one-size-fits-all model, promising a more effective and inclusive approach to education. Through GenAI-driven platforms, learning can become deeply personalized, catering to the unique pace, style, and interests of each student, and thereby maximizing their potential. Moreover, the ability of GenAI to revolutionize learning methodologies — from interactive virtual environments that facilitate experiential learning to AI-driven tutoring systems offering immediate feedback — enhances students' comprehension and fosters critical problem-solving skills.

Beyond transforming classroom learning, GenAI plays a pivotal role in promoting lifelong learning, enabling individuals to continue their educational journeys well beyond traditional settings and timelines. This adaptability is crucial for staying relevant in a rapidly evolving job market and society. Furthermore, GenAI's potential to democratize education, making high-quality learning experiences accessible to underserved communities, underscores its role in bridging educational divides and empowering a diverse range of learners.

However, the integration of GenAI into educational practices is not without its ethical and practical challenges. Issues such as data privacy, algorithmic bias, and ensuring equitable access to technology must be diligently addressed. Collaborative efforts among educators, policymakers, and technologists are vital in navigating these complexities, guiding the evolution of learning with GenAI towards principles of fairness, inclusivity, and respect for individual learners.

In summary, GenAI stands at the threshold of a new educational paradigm, offering significant opportunities to enhance how we learn and teach. As we embrace this era, our collective challenge is to deploy GenAI in a manner that fosters positive educational outcomes, ensuring that the future of learning is dynamic, inclusive, and reflective of the diverse needs and aspirations of all students.

Consequences

Certifications Become Obsolete

The realm of professional development and accreditation is poised for a seismic shift, largely catalyzed by the rise of GenAI. Long-standing hallmarks of professional attainment, such as Postgraduate Degrees and various certifications, are confronting an existential challenge. This transformation is spurred by several critical factors: the devaluation of certifications due to their proliferation, the superior educational offerings of GenAI, and mounting concerns over the integrity of certification exams.

The Proliferation Problem

The certification landscape has become increasingly crowded, with a vast array of credentials now available across numerous industries and skill levels. This glut has diluted the distinct value certifications once held, complicating the task for employers trying to discern genuinely skilled professionals from those who have merely amassed a collection of titles. This over-saturation has sparked a critical reassessment of the actual role and effectiveness of certifications in reliably denoting competence and expertise.

GenAI: The Superior Educator

The advent of GenAI as a transformative educational tool is reshaping this scenario. Unlike traditional certification training, often marked by a static, uniform approach, GenAI delivers personalized, adaptive learning experiences. It customizes educational content to match the learner's progress, preferences, and changing needs, fostering a more profound and practical comprehension of the subject matter. This dynamic, interactive mode of learning, facilitated by GenAI, challenges the relevance of conventional certification programs, which typically emphasize memorization and theoretical knowledge.

Integrity Issues in Certification

The integrity of certification exams has increasingly been called into question, echoing issues previously confined to academic examinations. Instances of cheating and obtaining certifications through dishonest means have cast a shadow over their credibility. In an era of easily accessible information and solutions, safeguarding the integrity of the certification process poses significant challenges, further eroding the trust in certifications as true reflections of an individual's skill and knowledge.

Rethinking Skill Validation

The convergence of these issues prompts a fundamental reevaluation of skill and expertise validation mechanisms in the professional sphere. If traditional certifications can no longer serve as definitive markers of competence, what alternatives might take their place? Emerging answers point towards a synergy of GenAI-driven education and innovative forms of skill assessment. Approaches such as portfolio reviews, contributions to real-world projects, and documented continuous learning, all enhanced by GenAI analytics, offer a more nuanced and accurate portrayal of an individual's capabilities and potential.

The Path Forward

The transition ahead necessitates a collaborative effort among educators, employers, and technology innovators to redefine norms for skill development and validation in a GenAI-influenced landscape. This requires not just the adoption of GenAI's educational potentials but also the creation of robust, equitable, and transparent methods for evaluating and acknowledging skills and expertise. These new models must prioritize maintaining integrity and public trust while accurately reflecting the competencies of the modern workforce.

The traditional higher education system, long celebrated as the pinnacle of intellectual achievement and a key to career success, is now teetering on the brink of a profound transformation. The rapid evolution of GenAI technologies and the shifting dynamics of the global job market highlight the potential decline of this revered institution. The challenges of adapting to technological advancements, the burgeoning crisis of student debt, and the diminishing value of many degrees underscore the urgent need for a reevaluation and reinvention of higher education.

The Pace of Technological Change

One of the most daunting challenges facing traditional higher education institutions is their inherent sluggishness in adapting to rapid technological changes. The lengthy processes involved in curriculum development, accreditation cycles, and the integration of academic research into teaching mean that educational content often becomes outdated before it even reaches students. In stark contrast, GenAI technologies evolve rapidly, continuously learning and innovating at a pace that far exceeds the capabilities of human instructors and traditional educational methods. This growing gap between the speed of technological advancement and the slow pace of educational adaptation casts doubt on the relevance and effectiveness of current higher education models in preparing students for the future workforce.

The Economic Equation

The economic model underpinning traditional higher education also faces significant scrutiny. Students frequently incur substantial debt, buoyed by the expectation that a degree will secure them better career opportunities and higher earnings. However, as the job market shifts toward valuing specific skills and competencies over formal educational credentials, many graduates find themselves either overqualified or working in fields unrelated to their degrees. The heavy burden of student loans, coupled with uncertain job prospects, challenges the notion that a traditional college degree is a sound investment in one's future.

The Value of Degrees

Moreover, in an era where specific, adaptable skills are increasingly valued over broad, theoretical knowledge, the relevance of many degrees is being questioned. As GenAI excels in areas such as data analysis and content creation, it exacerbates the skills gap, leaving graduates underprepared for a technology-driven job market. Employers are now prioritizing candidates who can adeptly navigate complex technological environments, adapt to new tools, and continuously update their skills in line with AI advancements. This shift demands a reevaluation of higher education's goals and the types of knowledge and skills it imparts to students.

Rethinking Higher Education

The looming collapse of traditional higher education is not an inevitability but a catalyst for radical change. It presents an opportunity to reimagine educational approaches to better align with the demands of the 21st century. This might involve integrating GenAI into educational frameworks, emphasizing skills-based learning, and adopting more adaptable, student-centric models that can swiftly respond to technological and economic shifts. Furthermore, exploring alternative credentialing methods, such as micro-credentials and digital portfolios, could provide more precise and relevant representations of an individual's skills and competencies.

The challenges confronting traditional higher education in the age of GenAI are significant, yet they also offer a unique chance to overhaul educational paradigms. By embracing innovation and critically assessing the foundational purposes of higher education, institutions can evolve to meet the needs of a rapidly changing world, ensuring their continued relevance and their role in developing the leaders, innovators, and thinkers of tomorrow. The potential decline of the traditional system serves as a pivotal warning that transformative change is not only necessary but imminent.

Chapter 8: A New Paradigm, Holistic Knowledge Validation

In an era where traditional certifications are becoming obsolete and lifelong learning emerges as the cornerstone of professional worth, the integration of GenAI offers a groundbreaking approach to validating knowledge and dedication to continuous education. This new paradigm, fueled by the capabilities of GenAI, shifts the focus from conventional credentials to a more comprehensive system of holistic knowledge validation. Here is how GenAI is redefining the landscape of educational achievement and professional qualifications:

Personalized Learning Pathways

The application of GenAI in creating personalized learning pathways offers a transformative shift in educational practices, ensuring that learning is highly individualized and deeply engaging. Here's how GenAI can be applied to achieve these personalized pathways:

Dynamic Content Adjustment

GenAI systems can analyze a learner's performance in real time and dynamically adjust the difficulty and type of content presented. For example, if a learner excels in a particular topic, the AI can introduce more complex materials or new, related subject areas to extend their learning. Conversely, if a learner struggles, the system can simplify the content or revisit foundational concepts to reinforce understanding. This responsive approach helps maintain an optimal learning curve and prevents learners from feeling overwhelmed or disengaged.

Continuous Feedback and Adaptation

Using machine learning algorithms, GenAI can provide continuous feedback to learners. This includes not only corrections and suggestions but also motivational feedback based on the learner's progress and interaction patterns. By continuously analyzing how learners respond to different teaching methods and materials, GenAI can further refine and personalize the learning experience, catering more precisely to the needs of each individual.

Integration of Interests and Goals

GenAI can incorporate a learner's personal interests and long-term educational or career goals into the learning pathway. By gathering data on the learner's engagement levels with various content types and subjects, GenAI can tailor the curriculum to include areas that pique the learner's interest, thereby enhancing motivation and engagement. For instance, if a learner shows a keen interest in environmental science, GenAI can integrate more content related to this field, even in subjects like mathematics or technology, illustrating practical applications that align with their interests.

Predictive Learning Interventions

With predictive analytics, GenAI can foresee potential challenges or learning blocks before they become significant issues. It can preemptively introduce supportive content or alternative learning strategies to address these challenges. For example, if a learner is likely to struggle with advanced mathematical concepts, GenAI can introduce supplementary materials or interactive tools to build competency in this area gradually.

Seamless Integration Across Platforms

GenAI can operate across various educational platforms and devices, providing a seamless and consistent learning experience. Whether a learner switches between a tablet, a laptop, or a smartphone, or moves from home study to a classroom environment, GenAI can synchronize learning progress and preferences across these platforms. This capability ensures that the learning journey is uninterrupted and consistently tailored to the learner's needs, regardless of the setting or device.

By leveraging these advanced capabilities, GenAI not only revolutionizes the way educational content is delivered and experienced but also places learners at the center of their educational journey. This approach not only improves learning outcomes by making education more relevant and engaging but also empowers learners to take control of their education, shaping it according to their unique needs, preferences, and future aspirations.

Dynamic Skill and Knowledge Validation with GenAI

GenAI revolutionizes the validation of skills and knowledge by moving beyond traditional, static assessments. It introduces dynamic, interactive methods that more accurately reflect real-world scenarios and challenges. Here's how GenAI can be applied to implement these advanced validation techniques:

Interactive Scenario-Based Assessments

GenAI can create complex, scenario-based simulations that require learners to apply their knowledge in contexts that mimic real-life situations. For instance, a GenAI system could simulate a business environment where a learner must make decisions based on fluctuating market data and limited resources, or a medical emergency where quick, informed action is necessary. These scenarios demand that learners not only recall information but also apply it creatively and effectively, providing a more comprehensive assessment of their capabilities.

Continuous, Real-Time Evaluation

Instead of relying on periodic tests, GenAI enables continuous evaluation through real-time interactions and tasks as learners engage with educational content. This ongoing assessment method allows for immediate feedback and adjustments to the learning pathway, helping learners correct misunderstandings and refine their skills continuously. This model of continuous assessment ensures that evaluations are up-to-date and reflect the learner's current abilities and knowledge.

Emphasis on Critical Thinking and Problem Solving

GenAI-driven evaluations prioritize critical thinking, problem-solving, and adaptability. By integrating these skills into assessments, GenAI ensures that learners are prepared for the unpredictability and rapid changes of the modern workplace. These assessments can dynamically adjust in complexity and nature, challenging learners to think on their feet and devise innovative solutions to novel problems.

Integration of Peer and Collaborative Assessment

GenAI can facilitate peer review and collaborative projects, where learners are evaluated on their ability to work with others, share ideas, and contribute to group tasks. This approach not only assesses individual knowledge and skills but also evaluates important interpersonal skills like communication, leadership, and teamwork. GenAI can analyze contributions and interactions within group settings to provide insights into each participant's performance and collaboration style.

Adaptability to Evolving Skill Sets

As job requirements evolve, the skills and knowledge considered valuable can shift. GenAI systems can quickly adapt assessments to reflect these changes, ensuring that evaluations remain relevant. This flexibility allows educational systems to keep pace with industry demands and provides learners with insights into emerging trends and necessary competencies.

Transparent and Fair Evaluation

To maintain trust in this new system, GenAI incorporates mechanisms to ensure that assessments are transparent and fair. This includes clear explanations of how decisions are made and providing learners with detailed feedback on their performance. It also involves regular audits of the AI algorithms to detect and correct any biases that may affect the fairness of evaluations.

By employing these dynamic methods, GenAI transforms how skills and knowledge are validated, making the process more reflective of actual workplace requirements and more responsive to the individual needs and abilities of learners. This shift promises not only to enhance the relevance and accuracy of assessments but also to better prepare learners for the complexities of the modern world.

Continuous Feedback and Growth with GenAI

The integration of GenAI into the educational process, particularly in providing instant and continuous feedback, fundamentally transforms how learning is approached. This innovative use of GenAI creates a dynamic environment where feedback is not episodic but a constant dialogue, enhancing both the acquisition of knowledge and the personal development of learners. Here's a deeper look at how continuous feedback from GenAI can facilitate ongoing growth and learning:

Instant Feedback on Performance

GenAI can assess learners' inputs immediately, providing instant feedback on assignments, quizzes, and interactive tasks. This immediate response allows learners to understand what they've mastered and where they need more focus, adjusting their learning paths accordingly in real-time. For instance, if a learner struggles with a specific concept in mathematics, GenAI can provide tailored practice questions and explanatory content to address these gaps.

Identifying Strengths and Areas for Improvement

By continuously analyzing the learner's performance and engagement, GenAI can identify patterns that highlight both strengths and weaknesses. This ongoing assessment helps learners and educators understand which areas are well-developed and which require additional attention, allowing for a more targeted and effective educational approach. This process not only enhances learning efficiency but also helps build learners' confidence in their abilities while clearly mapping out areas for further development.

Fostering a Lifelong Learning Mindset

The perpetual feedback provided by GenAI encourages learners to adopt a mindset of lifelong learning. With constant updates on their progress and continual challenges presented based on their skill level, learners are motivated to keep improving and expanding their knowledge base. This system helps inculcate the habit of continuous personal and professional development, essential in today's rapidly changing world.

Personalized Learning Experiences

GenAI's feedback mechanisms are highly personalized, taking into account the individual learner's pace, style, and preferences. This customization makes learning more engaging and effective, as learners feel that the educational content is specifically tailored to them. For example, if a learner shows a keen interest in a particular topic, GenAI can provide additional, more in-depth resources to foster that curiosity, further enhancing motivation.

Encouraging Self-Reflection

Continuous feedback from GenAI also promotes self-reflection among learners. By regularly receiving insights into their learning habits and outcomes, learners are encouraged to think critically about their own educational processes, what works best for them, and how they can apply their learning more effectively in practical contexts.

Building Resilience and Adaptability

The regular feedback provided by GenAI helps learners build resilience by normalizing the learning process as a cycle of trial, error, and improvement. This approach reduces the stigma associated with making mistakes, instead framing challenges as opportunities for growth and learning. It also enhances learners' adaptability, preparing them to respond flexibly to feedback and apply new strategies to their learning and problem-solving efforts.

In summary, the power of GenAI to provide continuous feedback revolutionizes the educational landscape by transforming feedback into an ongoing, interactive dialogue that enhances learning, fosters personal growth, and encourages a lifelong commitment to learning. Through this dynamic interaction, learners are continually motivated to refine their skills and expand their knowledge, preparing them for the complexities of the modern professional and personal life.

The Digital Portfolio: An Immutable Ledger of Achievement

In the evolving landscape of professional and educational validation, GenAI paves the way for the digital portfolio—an immutable ledger that encapsulates an individual's comprehensive learning milestones, achievements, and contributions. This dynamic, AI-managed portfolio transcends the limitations of traditional resumes and certificates, providing a holistic and continuously updated record of a person's educational and professional journey. Here's how GenAI transforms personal achievement records through the digital portfolio:

Comprehensive Record Keeping

A digital portfolio curated by GenAI integrates data from a wide array of sources to compile a detailed record of an individual's learning and achievements. Unlike static resumes, this digital portfolio includes formal educational qualifications, informal learning experiences, professional accomplishments, and even personal creative projects. It offers a complete view that reflects not just the outcomes but also the process of learning and development.

Authentication and Validation by AI

Each entry in the digital portfolio is authenticated and continuously updated by GenAI, ensuring that the information is accurate and current. GenAI can verify achievements and credentials by cross-referencing data from educational institutions, workplaces, and other credible sources. This process enhances the integrity of the portfolio, making it a reliable source of information for potential employers, educational institutions, and collaborators.

Dynamic Updates and Personalization

As individuals continue to learn and achieve, the digital portfolio is dynamically updated to reflect new skills, knowledge, and experiences. GenAI algorithms personalize the presentation of the portfolio based on the context in which it is viewed, emphasizing relevant accomplishments and skills that align with specific job opportunities or educational programs. This targeted approach maximizes the portfolio's impact and relevance.

Accessibility and Shareability

The digital portfolio, hosted on a secure, cloud-based platform, can be easily accessed and shared with potential employers, academic admissions committees, or even peers seeking collaboration. The immutable nature of the ledger ensures that once achievements are verified and added, they cannot be tampered with, maintaining the portfolio's credibility and trustworthiness.

Encouraging Lifelong Learning

The digital portfolio encourages individuals to engage in lifelong learning by visually representing their growth and learning trajectory. Seeing one's achievements and progress cataloged over time can be highly motivating, pushing individuals to continue seeking new learning opportunities and experiences to add to their portfolios.

Ethical Considerations and Privacy

While the digital portfolio offers numerous benefits, it also raises important ethical considerations, particularly regarding data privacy and security. It is crucial to implement stringent security measures to protect sensitive information and ensure that individuals have control over who can access their portfolios. Additionally, ethical use of AI in curating and updating these portfolios must be ensured to prevent biases and ensure fairness in how information is represented and utilized.

In conclusion, the digital portfolio, facilitated by GenAI, represents a significant innovation in how individual achievements and learning are documented and shared. This digital, immutable ledger not only provides a more complete picture of an individual's capabilities and experiences but also aligns with the future of work and education, where continuous learning and adaptability are key.

Authenticating Holistic Knowledge

GenAI serves a pivotal function in the authentication of holistic knowledge within digital portfolios, ensuring that every piece of information is securely validated and maintained in a verifiable format. This robust system not only guarantees the integrity and accuracy of the recorded data but also establishes a transparent and tamper-proof foundation for evaluating an individual's professional and educational development. Here's how GenAI enhances the authentication process:

Verifiable Data Integrity

GenAI systems utilize advanced cryptographic techniques to secure and authenticate data entries in digital portfolios. This involves creating digital signatures for each entry, which confirm the authenticity and immutability of the information. By integrating blockchain technology or similar decentralized ledger systems, GenAI ensures that once an achievement or credential is recorded, it cannot be altered or falsified without detection.

Continuous Validation

Beyond initial authentication, GenAI continuously validates the entries in a digital portfolio by cross-referencing them with external data sources, such as educational institutions, certification bodies, and workplace databases. This ongoing verification process helps to maintain the portfolio's relevance and trustworthiness, ensuring that all listed credentials and achievements remain valid and are represented accurately over time.

Transparency in Record-Keeping

GenAI contributes to creating a highly transparent record-keeping system where the origins and verification status of each portfolio entry are openly accessible to authorized viewers. This transparency is crucial for building trust among potential employers, educational institutions, and collaborators who rely on the portfolio for decision-making purposes. It allows them to verify the authenticity of the information directly, fostering confidence in the portfolio holder's capabilities and achievements.

Protection Against Fraud

With its capability to authenticate and securely store data, GenAI plays a critical role in protecting against fraud and misrepresentation in digital portfolios. By ensuring that all entries are verified and tamper-proof, GenAI minimizes the risk of fraudulent claims, which can undermine the credibility of traditional resumes and certificates. This protection is particularly important in competitive job markets and high-stakes academic applications, where the accuracy of one's credentials can significantly impact opportunities.

Facilitating Professional and Educational Growth

By providing a secure, authenticated record of an individual's learning and achievements, GenAI empowers individuals to pursue a proactive approach to their professional and educational growth. The clarity and reliability of the information within digital portfolios make it easier for individuals to identify areas for improvement, seek out relevant learning opportunities, and strategically plan their career development based on verified skills and knowledge.

Conclusion of Chapter 10: A New Paradigm, Holistic Knowledge Validation

As we conclude Chapter 10, it is clear that the integration of GenAI into educational and professional validation represents a profound shift from traditional methods. This new paradigm, driven by the capabilities of GenAI, not only challenges the status quo but also opens up expansive opportunities for individuals to demonstrate their competencies in more dynamic and authentic ways.

The obsolescence of traditional certifications and degrees, once seen as the gold standards of educational and professional achievement, underscores the need for a system that can keep pace with the rapid advancements in technology and the evolving demands of the global job market. GenAI offers a promising solution by enabling the creation of personalized learning pathways that adapt to individual needs and pacing, ensuring that education is a continuous, engaging, and deeply personalized experience.

Moreover, the shift towards dynamic validation of skills and knowledge through GenAI-powered systems highlights a critical evolution in how we assess competencies. Interactive scenarios, real-world applications, and continuous feedback mechanisms provide a richer, more accurate picture of an individual's abilities, emphasizing practical skills over theoretical knowledge. This approach not only enhances learning outcomes but also better prepares individuals for the complexities and challenges of modern professional environments.

The development of digital portfolios as immutable ledgers of achievement is particularly noteworthy. These portfolios offer a comprehensive and verifiable record of an individual's learning journey, showcasing not only formal education but also informal learning, personal projects, and professional experiences. This holistic view of achievement, authenticated and continuously updated by GenAI, provides a more nuanced and complete picture of an individual's capabilities and growth over time.

As we look to the future, the role of educators, employers, and technology developers will be crucial in fully realizing the potential of this new paradigm. Collaboration among these stakeholders is essential to refine these tools, address ethical and practical challenges, and ensure that the benefits of GenAI are accessible to all. It is also imperative to foster an environment that values continuous learning, adaptability, and the nuanced understanding of skills and knowledge that GenAI facilitates.

In embracing this new paradigm of holistic knowledge validation, we are not just adapting to technological changes—we are also taking a significant step towards a more inclusive, equitable, and effective system of education and professional development. This transformation, while complex, promises to empower individuals and enrich societies, paving the way for a future where education and professional validation are truly reflective of an individual's abilities and potential to contribute meaningfully to their fields.

Part III: Economic and Social Impacts

Chapter 9: The New Economic Landscape

In the evolving landscape of knowledge and innovation, AI technologies, particularly GenAI, play a pivotal role in uncovering previously unexplored or under-researched domains within law, regulations, and academic research. This capability of AI to identify gaps and opportunities in existing bodies of knowledge not only challenges our understanding of these fields but also opens new avenues for publishing and research. This chapter delves into how AI's unique insights can transform these critical areas, highlighting the potential for groundbreaking work and the expansion of human understanding.

"AI has the potential to revolutionize legal research. By analyzing vast amounts of case law and legal documents, AI can identify patterns and connections that humans might miss. This could lead to more nuanced and precise legal interpretations." Leora Morgenstern, Professor of Law and Computer Science, Northeastern University.

AI as the Cartographer of Knowledge

GenAI serves as an advanced cartographer in the vast and often uncharted territories of knowledge across various disciplines. Its ability to analyze large datasets and uncover patterns or anomalies plays a crucial role in mapping existing knowledge while also revealing gaps and opportunities for further exploration. This section delves deeper into how GenAI acts as a sophisticated tool for navigating and expanding the frontiers of legal, regulatory, and academic knowledge.

Deep Data Analysis

GenAI's strength lies in its capacity to process and synthesize information from extensive and diverse data sources rapidly. In the context of legal and regulatory frameworks, GenAI can scan through decades of case law, statutes, and legal commentary to identify trends and precedents that might escape even the most diligent researchers. This deep analysis allows GenAI to construct a detailed map of the legal landscape, highlighting well-trodden paths and neglected areas that may require more scholarly attention or legislative review.

Identifying Contradictions and Ambiguities

One of the most valuable aspects of using GenAI in knowledge mapping is its ability to detect inconsistencies and ambiguities within the existing body of work. By cross-referencing multiple sources and jurisdictions, GenAI can pinpoint discrepancies in legal opinions or regulatory guidelines that may lead to confusion or misinterpretation. These findings are crucial for legal scholars, policymakers, and practitioners who strive to create more coherent and universally applicable legal frameworks.

Uncovering Knowledge Gaps

GenAI not only maps what is known but also shines a light on what is missing. In academic research, this involves analyzing existing literature and datasets to identify areas that lack empirical support or theoretical development. For instance, in environmental law, GenAI might reveal a lack of research on the long-term effects of certain regulations on biodiversity, suggesting a need for comprehensive studies in this area. These insights can guide funding bodies, academic institutions, and researchers in prioritizing projects and resources.

Fostering Interdisciplinary Research

The ability of GenAI to integrate and analyze data from various fields can facilitate the emergence of interdisciplinary research areas that combine insights from multiple disciplines. For example, GenAI might link findings from environmental science with public health to propose new areas of study in environmental health policy. By breaking down the silos that traditionally separate different fields of study, GenAI encourages a more holistic approach to research that reflects the complex, interconnected nature of real-world issues.

Enhancing Regulatory Oversight

In the realm of regulations, GenAI's detailed mapping of existing policies and their impacts can assist regulators in identifying outdated rules or areas where new regulations are necessary. By providing a comprehensive overview of the regulatory landscape, GenAI helps ensure that oversight keeps pace with technological and social changes, thereby enhancing the effectiveness and relevance of regulatory frameworks.

Transforming Legal Scholarship and Practice

"AI offers tremendous potential for legal research, enabling lawyers to analyze vast amounts of legal documents and case law more efficiently and identify relevant precedents previously missed." - Margaret Greer (Law Professor at Stanford Law School)

In the realm of law, the impact of AI, particularly GenAI, is revolutionizing how legal scholarship and practice are approached. By identifying under-explored areas within legal domains, GenAI provides a unique opportunity for legal scholars and practitioners to expand the boundaries of current knowledge and adapt to the evolving demands of society and technology. Here's a deeper look into how GenAI is driving this transformative change:

Unveiling New Legal Theories

GenAI's ability to process vast arrays of legal documents and data allows it to identify patterns and gaps that might not be apparent through traditional research methods. This capability enables legal scholars to discover under-researched areas that may hold the key to developing new legal theories. By analyzing historical legal data, contemporary case law, and statutory materials, GenAI can suggest correlations and trends that prompt a reevaluation of existing legal frameworks and the formulation of innovative legal theories that better address current realities.

Examining Regulations in Light of Emerging Technologies

As technology rapidly advances, existing regulations often struggle to keep pace. GenAI assists in this regard by analyzing the implications of emerging technologies on current regulatory frameworks. For instance, issues such as data privacy, cybersecurity, and the ethical use of AI in various sectors present complex challenges that existing laws may not adequately address. GenAI can help legal experts identify these regulatory gaps and work towards developing laws that effectively govern new technologies while protecting societal interests.

Exploring Jurisprudence in Evolving Societal Contexts

Society is in a constant state of flux, influenced by economic shifts, cultural transformations, and technological advancements. GenAI plays a crucial role in exploring how jurisprudence can evolve in response to these changes. By providing insights into societal trends and their legal implications, GenAI enables legal scholars and practitioners to consider how laws can be interpreted or evolved to better serve the changing needs of society. This might involve reassessing legal doctrines in light of societal attitudes towards issues like privacy, work, and human rights.

Enabling Publishers to Fill Knowledge Gaps

For legal publishers, the insights provided by GenAI represent valuable opportunities to commission works that fill identified gaps in legal scholarship. By highlighting under-explored areas, GenAI guides publishers to areas where demand for new knowledge is high but supply is low. This not only contributes to the advancement of legal knowledge but also helps legal professionals stay ahead of the curve, ensuring that their practices remain relevant and effective in a rapidly changing legal landscape.

Facilitating Continuous Legal Education

GenAI also enhances the continuing education of legal professionals by providing up-to-date, relevant content tailored to the needs of the legal community. Through seminars, workshops, and online courses that incorporate the latest GenAI findings, legal professionals can continuously update their knowledge and skills. This ongoing education is essential for lawyers, judges, and other legal practitioners to effectively interpret and apply law in dynamic and complex scenarios.

Impact on Legal Practice

The integration of GenAI into legal scholarship and practice is not just about enhancing legal research; it's about transforming the very fabric of how law is studied, interpreted, and applied. By driving a more dynamic, responsive, and informed legal practice, GenAI helps ensure that the law not only keeps pace with but anticipates and shapes societal progress.

Revolutionizing Regulatory Analysis

Regulations, designed to keep pace with technological and social changes, often lag behind the rapid evolution of society. AI's capability to highlight areas of regulations that are outdated, inconsistent, or lacking provides regulators, policymakers, and scholars with critical insights. This intelligence can guide the revision of existing regulations and the creation of new frameworks that better reflect current realities. For academic and professional publishers, this opens up a demand for publications that analyze, critique, and propose innovations in regulatory policies.

Catalyzing New Research Directions

"AI's ability to analyze massive datasets and identify complex patterns can spark entirely new research questions and areas of scientific inquiry." - Dr. Patricia Culliane (Director of the National Science Foundation's AI Directorate)

GenAI is proving to be a transformative force in the field of academic research, offering unprecedented capabilities to enhance the scope and depth of scholarly inquiry. By efficiently mining and analyzing global research outputs, GenAI identifies not only existing knowledge gaps but also suggests fertile areas for future studies. Here's how GenAI is catalyzing new research directions and fostering interdisciplinary innovation:

Identifying Knowledge Gaps

GenAI algorithms can process extensive databases of academic literature, identifying patterns, trends, and, importantly, areas lacking sufficient research. This capability allows researchers to pinpoint specific topics within their fields that require deeper investigation, ensuring that their efforts are both necessary and contributive to the broader academic community. By highlighting these gaps, GenAI helps avoid redundancy in research efforts and directs attention to where it is most needed.

Proposing Interdisciplinary Research Questions

One of GenAI's most significant impacts is its ability to suggest research questions that bridge multiple disciplines, fostering a holistic approach to solving complex problems. For example, GenAI might analyze data from environmental science and public health to propose studies on the impact of pollution on human health, or it could combine insights from psychology and technology to explore the effects of social media on mental well-being. These interdisciplinary approaches are increasingly important as global challenges become more intricate and interconnected.

Developing Novel Methodologies

GenAI doesn't just identify what to study; it also suggests how to study it. By recognizing patterns and correlations within vast datasets, GenAI can propose novel methodologies that are more efficient, accurate, or comprehensive. This might involve innovative data collection techniques, new models for statistical analysis, or even the development of new tools for data visualization. These methodologies can significantly enhance the robustness and impact of research findings.

Highlighting Societal Challenges

GenAI is particularly adept at analyzing data from a variety of sources to identify broader societal challenges that require academic attention. This may include emerging public health crises, unaddressed environmental issues, or underexplored economic inequalities. By bringing these issues to the forefront, GenAI ensures that academic research is closely aligned with societal needs and contributes effectively to public discourse and policy-making.

Informing Publishers and Driving Cutting-Edge Publications

The insights provided by GenAI are invaluable for academic publishers. By informing them about emerging trends and unexplored areas of research, GenAI helps publishers stay ahead of the curve, encouraging them to commission works that address these new and vital topics. This not only drives the publication of innovative and timely research but also helps shape the academic agenda, steering the intellectual focus of entire disciplines towards areas with high potential for impact.

Enhancing the Impact of Academic Research

Overall, GenAI's role in catalyzing new research directions revitalizes the academic landscape, making it more dynamic, responsive, and integrated. By leveraging GenAI's capabilities, researchers can push the boundaries of knowledge, tackle more complex problems, and produce research that is both innovative and highly relevant to contemporary challenges. This ongoing evolution in academic research driven by GenAI not only enriches scholarly work but also significantly contributes to the progress and well-being of society.

Publishers, Researchers, and Fact-Checkers: Embracing AI's Revelations

"The rise of deepfakes and other forms of synthetic media necessitates the development of more sophisticated AI tools for fact-checking. Collaboration between fact-checkers and AI developers is crucial for maintaining a reliable information landscape." - Claire Dubois (Journalist and Fact-Checking Specialist)

For publishers, researchers, and fact-checkers, the insights provided by AI, particularly GenAI, necessitate a proactive and visionary approach to their work. As AI continues to unveil new realms of uncharted knowledge, these professionals are called upon to not only acknowledge but actively engage with these revelations. Here's a deeper exploration of how AI is reshaping their roles and encouraging a collaborative approach to knowledge discovery and validation:

Proactive Engagement with AI Insights

Publishers and researchers must be willing to venture beyond traditional boundaries and explore topics that AI identifies as under-researched or potentially groundbreaking. This might involve investing in research areas that have not yet gained mainstream attention but have the potential to address critical gaps in knowledge or introduce innovative perspectives. For instance, AI might highlight a burgeoning issue in environmental science that could have profound implications for sustainability practices, prompting publishers to seek out experts who can contribute deeper insights on the subject.

Collaborative Efforts Across Disciplines

The nature of AI's insights often transcends conventional disciplinary boundaries, suggesting connections between seemingly disparate fields. This calls for a collaborative approach among professionals from various domains. AI technologists, legal experts, regulatory bodies, and members of the academic community must work together to fully explore and understand these connections. Such collaboration can lead to more comprehensive and multifaceted research outcomes, enhancing the richness and applicability of scholarly work.

Fact-Checkers and AI: A Partnership for Accuracy

Fact-checkers play a critical role in verifying the accuracy of information before it reaches wider audiences, a task that is becoming increasingly complex with the rapid dissemination of data and research findings. AI tools can assist fact-checkers by quickly scanning large volumes of content to identify inconsistencies or claims that require verification. This partnership can significantly enhance the efficiency and effectiveness of fact-checking processes, ensuring that published content is both accurate and trustworthy.

Investment in AI-Driven Research

To fully capitalize on AI's potential, publishers and research institutions may need to invest in AI technologies and expertise. This includes training for researchers and editorial staff to effectively use AI tools in their work, and funding for AI-driven research projects that push the boundaries of traditional methodologies. Investing in AI not only enhances the scope and impact of research but also positions institutions at the forefront of innovation in their respective fields.

Ethical Considerations and Responsibility

As researchers and publishers delve deeper into AI-driven insights, they must also navigate the ethical implications of using AI in their work. This includes considerations around data privacy, the potential biases in AI algorithms, and the societal impact of their research. Ensuring that AI is used responsibly and ethically is crucial for maintaining public trust and upholding the integrity of the research process.

The integration of AI into the fields of publishing, research, and fact-checking is transforming these disciplines in profound ways. By embracing AI's ability to map uncharted territories of knowledge, professionals in these fields can unlock new opportunities for discovery and impact. However, realizing this potential requires not only technological investment but also a commitment to collaboration, ethical practice, and continual adaptation to the evolving landscape of knowledge and technology.

Revolutionizing Patent Searches

"AI can help identify potential patent infringements and prior art that might have been missed by traditional searches. This is crucial for businesses looking to protect their intellectual property and avoid legal issues." - Sarah Jones (Intellectual Property Lawyer)

The advent of GenAI is set to transform the realm of patent law, reshaping the methodologies and strategies of patent filing, litigation, and overall intellectual property management. GenAI's capability to sift through extensive databases of patent information, legal precedents, and technical documentation provides an unprecedented opportunity to enhance and innovate within the patent landscape. Here, we explore how GenAI could revolutionize various aspects of patent law, from streamlining patent searches to identifying underexplored domains for innovation.

Automating Comprehensive Patent Searches

GenAI revolutionizes the way patent searches are conducted by automating the review process of existing patents, legal literature, and technical documents. Its ability to analyze complex technical information and extract relevant data can significantly expedite the patent search process. This automation ensures that inventors and companies can navigate the patent landscape more effectively, reducing the time and resources required for comprehensive searches and minimizing the risks of infringement.

Enhancing Patent Drafting

Drafting patent applications is a complex process that requires high precision and a deep understanding of specific technical domains. GenAI can assist in this process by suggesting optimal language and structure for patent applications, drawing from a database of successfully granted patents in related fields. This support helps ensure that patent applications are robust, articulate the novelty of the invention clearly, and meet the stringent requirements of patent offices, thereby increasing the likelihood of obtaining patent approvals.

Identifying Underexplored Domains

One of the most compelling uses of GenAI in patent law is its ability to identify gaps and opportunities within the existing patent landscape. By analyzing trends, technological advancements, and the density of patents across various sectors, GenAI can pinpoint areas ripe for innovation. This guidance can direct researchers and inventors towards these less saturated areas, where they have higher chances of developing novel inventions and securing intellectual property rights.

Predictive Analysis for Patent Litigation

GenAI also offers predictive insights that can reshape patent litigation strategies. By evaluating historical case law, challenges to patent validity, and litigation trends, GenAI can forecast likely outcomes of patent disputes. This predictive capability allows patent holders and litigants to make more informed decisions regarding whether to initiate, settle, or defend against litigation, based on predicted success rates.

Streamlining Patent Portfolio Management

For organizations with extensive patent portfolios, GenAI provides tools to analyze and strategically manage these assets. By assessing the strength, relevance, and commercial potential of each patent, GenAI can aid companies in making informed decisions about maintaining, licensing, or divesting patents. This strategic management helps align the patent portfolio with broader business goals, optimizing the value of intellectual property assets.

Challenges and Ethical Considerations

The integration of GenAI into patent law is not without its challenges. Issues such as data privacy, potential biases in AI algorithms, and the ethical implications of AI-generated inventions must be addressed. It is crucial to maintain transparency in the decision-making processes of GenAI systems, ensure human oversight in critical decisions, and develop comprehensive ethical guidelines for the deployment of AI in patent-related activities.

Reconfiguring Productivity

GenAI stands at the forefront of a productivity revolution. By automating complex tasks, from data analysis to content creation, it enables a leap in efficiency and output previously unimaginable. Businesses harnessing GenAI can achieve more with less, pushing the boundaries of productivity and fostering innovation at an unprecedented pace. This surge in productivity has the potential to drive economic growth, stimulate new industries, and redefine competitive dynamics across sectors.

However, the benefits of this productivity boom are contingent on equitable access to GenAI technologies and the capacity of industries to adapt. The disparity in access and adaptation could exacerbate existing economic inequalities, underscoring the need for policies that foster inclusive growth and widespread adoption of GenAI innovations.

Transforming the Job Market

The impact of GenAI on the job market is profound and dual-faceted. On one hand, it heralds the automation of routine and repetitive tasks, challenging traditional employment models and necessitating a reevaluation of skills valued in the workforce. Occupations heavily reliant on tasks that can be automated by GenAI face the risk of obsolescence, prompting a wave of job displacement.

On the other hand, GenAI also creates new opportunities, giving rise to jobs that manage, interpret, and innovate upon AI-generated outputs. The demand for skills in AI ethics, data analysis, and human-AI interaction design is set to soar, reflecting the evolving needs of a GenAI-driven economy. Furthermore, GenAI's role in augmenting human capabilities opens avenues for enhanced creativity and innovation, suggesting that the future job market will highly prize interdisciplinary skills, adaptability, and continuous learning.

Redefining the Concept of Work

Perhaps most fundamentally, GenAI challenges and redefines the concept of work itself. Work in the GenAI era transcends traditional boundaries, blurring the lines between human and machine contributions. This new paradigm necessitates a shift in how work is valued and compensated, with implications for everything from wage structures to intellectual property rights.

Moreover, GenAI's capacity to personalize and enhance learning fosters a culture of lifelong education, where the acquisition of new skills and adaptation to changing technologies become integral to professional life. This continuous learning environment, supported by GenAI, can democratize access to knowledge and skills, reshaping career trajectories and enabling individuals to navigate the changing job market more fluidly.

Navigating the Transition

The transition to a GenAI-driven economic landscape presents both challenges and opportunities. Policymakers, educators, and business leaders play pivotal roles in shaping this transition, ensuring that the economic benefits of GenAI are broadly shared and that workers displaced by automation have pathways to new opportunities. Investment in education, training programs, and policies that encourage innovation while protecting against inequality will be crucial in realizing the positive potential of GenAI in the economy.

Conclusion

As we conclude this Chapter, it is evident that GenAI is reshaping the economic and intellectual landscapes in profound ways, particularly within the realms of law, regulations, and academic research. This transformative technology is not just altering how knowledge is discovered and utilized; it is also redefining the structures of industries that depend heavily on intellectual and regulatory agility.

GenAI acts as a powerful catalyst in identifying gaps and opportunities in vast domains of knowledge, thereby pushing the boundaries of what is possible in legal and academic research. By serving as a sophisticated cartographer of knowledge, GenAI not only maps out existing information but also points to the unexplored, sometimes revealing critical areas that require attention or promise significant breakthroughs.

The economic implications of such insights are substantial. GenAI drives efficiency, reducing costs and time in data processing and analysis, which is especially transformative in fields like patent law and regulatory compliance. These efficiencies translate into economic gains for businesses and institutions by streamlining operations and enhancing the strategic management of intellectual properties.

Moreover, the social implications of integrating GenAI are profound. This technology democratizes access to complex information, making it possible for a wider audience to engage with and influence fields previously gated by expertise and resources. As GenAI continues to break down these barriers, it fosters a more inclusive intellectual ecosystem where diverse perspectives can contribute to and benefit from advanced research and development.

However, the journey ahead is not without its challenges. The ethical considerations surrounding GenAI—such as data privacy, algorithmic bias, and the integrity of AI-generated content—require diligent attention and proactive management. The success of GenAI in reshaping the economic landscape will depend not only on technological advancements but also on our ability to navigate these ethical dilemmas responsibly.

Chapter 10: The GenAI Era, cutting through the complexity of Cross Disciplinary Discoveries.

Biomimicry and Materials Science

Biomimicry, the practice of drawing inspiration from nature to solve human challenges, has been a fertile ground for innovations across various fields, particularly in materials science. With the advent of GenAI, the potential for groundbreaking advancements in this area is significantly amplified. GenAI can accelerate the discovery and application of biomimetic solutions by harnessing its vast data-processing capabilities and deep learning algorithms to explore and interpret nature's designs in ways previously unimaginable. Here's a deeper look at how GenAI is poised to transform biomimicry and materials science:

Enhanced Discovery of Biological Mechanisms

GenAI can analyze extensive datasets from biological research to identify structures and mechanisms that have proven effective in the natural world but have not yet been studied or applied in technological contexts. For instance, the architecture of bone, which provides maximum strength with minimal weight, or the self-healing capabilities of certain plants, could inspire the development of advanced building materials or self-repairing polymers. GenAI's ability to sift through and make connections from vast amounts of biological data can uncover these natural secrets more rapidly and comprehensively than traditional research methods.

Simulation and Modeling

With advanced simulation capabilities, GenAI can model how natural structures might be replicated or adapted in materials science. This involves not only direct emulation of natural properties but also the modification and optimization of these properties to meet specific human needs. For example, the branching patterns of trees and plants for maximum sunlight capture could inspire more efficient layouts for solar panels or enhance the design of urban spaces for improved light distribution and energy efficiency.

Predictive Analysis for Material Innovation

GenAI's predictive capabilities allow it to forecast the potential success and functionality of new materials inspired by biomimicry. By analyzing existing data on material properties and performance, alongside environmental and operational conditions, GenAI can predict how biomimetic materials might perform in real-world applications. This predictive analysis is invaluable in guiding research priorities and investment decisions, ensuring that efforts are focused on the most promising innovations.

Cross-disciplinary Integration

GenAI facilitates greater integration between biology and materials science, often bringing together experts from these traditionally separate fields to collaborate on biomimetic projects. This cross-disciplinary approach is essential as it combines deep insights from biology with the practical applications of materials science, leading to more innovative and effective solutions. GenAI serves as a bridge, enhancing communication and understanding between these experts, and speeding up the iterative process of design and testing.

Real-World Applications

The potential applications of biomimetic materials are vast and varied. From creating antimicrobial surfaces inspired by shark skin to developing new aerospace materials that mimic the lightweight and robust characteristics of bird bones, the opportunities for innovation are boundless. GenAI not only aids in the discovery and development of these materials but also helps in identifying the most suitable applications for new technologies, optimizing their impact and usability in society.

Environmental Science and Urban Planning

As urban populations continue to expand, the integration of sustainable development principles into urban planning is becoming increasingly crucial. GenAI stands to revolutionize this integration by harnessing environmental science insights to create more sustainable, resilient, and livable urban environments. Here's how GenAI could transform urban planning through a deep understanding of environmental science:

Data-Driven Urban Design

GenAI can analyze vast amounts of data related to ecosystem services, biodiversity, and climate regulation to inform urban design. By understanding the specific needs and capacities of different ecosystems, GenAI can help urban planners create designs that enhance green spaces, promote biodiversity, and foster sustainable interactions between urban and natural environments. This could involve the strategic placement of green roofs, parks, and green corridors that connect larger ecosystems, helping to maintain biodiversity and ecosystem services within urban settings.

Climate Resilience and Sustainability

One of the critical roles GenAI can play in urban planning is enhancing climate resilience. By processing historical climate data and current climate models, GenAI can identify patterns and predict future climate-related challenges specific to different regions. This information is invaluable for urban planners aiming to design cities that can withstand changing climate conditions, manage extreme weather events, and mitigate the effects of heat islands, flooding, and droughts. GenAI might suggest incorporating permeable surfaces, enhanced drainage systems, and flood barriers that are tailored to the city's specific climate challenges.

Water Management Innovations

Drawing inspiration from natural water management systems, such as the rainwater harvesting techniques observed in forest ecosystems, GenAI could revolutionize urban water management strategies. It can offer designs for cities that mimic these natural systems, potentially reducing water scarcity issues and mitigating flood risks. For example, GenAI could help plan urban landscapes that integrate rain gardens, bioswales, and artificial wetlands, which naturally filter and redirect rainwater, reducing runoff and enhancing water quality.

Optimizing Resource Efficiency

GenAI's capability to optimize resource allocation is particularly beneficial in urban planning. By analyzing patterns of energy consumption, waste generation, and resource distribution, GenAI can propose more efficient models for resource management in urban settings. This might include smart energy grids that dynamically adjust to energy demands or waste recycling systems that are both environmentally friendly and economically viable.

Engaging Public Participation

Finally, GenAI can facilitate greater public engagement in urban planning processes by making complex data and plans more accessible to the general public. Interactive AI-driven platforms can visualize potential urban plans and allow citizens to input their preferences and feedback, making the urban planning process more inclusive and democratic. This can help ensure that the development plans align more closely with the needs and values of the community, fostering a sense of ownership and responsibility towards sustainable urban development.

Impact on Urban Development

The integration of GenAI into urban planning signifies a transformative leap forward in the construction of smarter, more sustainable cities. This technology's potential to harness vast amounts of environmental science data and insights allows urban planners to design cities that harmonize human habitation with environmental sustainability and resilience. Here's a deeper exploration of how GenAI influences urban development:

Advancing Sustainable Urban Design

GenAI enables the design and implementation of urban areas that prioritize sustainability. By analyzing data on environmental impact, resource usage, and human activity patterns, GenAI can help design cities that optimize energy efficiency, reduce waste, and promote ecological balance. Features like green roofs, energy-efficient buildings, and integrated natural habitats can become standard in urban landscapes, reducing the ecological footprint of cities and enhancing their sustainability.

Enhancing Climate Resilience

Climate resilience is a critical consideration for future urban development, and GenAI offers significant advancements in this area. By predicting climate trends and assessing potential risks, GenAI enables urban planners to implement proactive measures to withstand environmental stressors. This might include flood defenses, heatwave mitigation strategies like cool roofs and shaded walkways, and infrastructure designed to withstand extreme weather events. These measures ensure that cities are better equipped to handle the challenges posed by climate change, protecting residents and minimizing potential damage.

Improving Quality of Life

GenAI-driven urban planning directly contributes to enhancing the quality of life for city dwellers. By creating more livable and enjoyable urban environments that offer clean air, abundant green spaces, and efficient public services, GenAI helps make cities more attractive places to live. Additionally, GenAI can optimize traffic flow, reduce noise pollution, and enhance public safety, further improving urban living conditions.

Promoting Inclusive and Equitable Development

GenAI also plays a crucial role in ensuring that urban development is inclusive and equitable. By analyzing demographic data and community feedback, GenAI can help identify and address the needs of diverse urban populations. This includes designing accessible public spaces, ensuring equitable distribution of resources like parks and schools, and tailoring services to meet the specific needs of different community groups. As a result, GenAI contributes to creating cities that serve all their residents fairly and effectively.

Facilitating Continuous Improvement and Adaptation

Urban development is not a static process, and GenAI supports the continuous improvement and adaptation of urban environments. Through ongoing monitoring and data analysis, GenAI can provide urban planners with real-time feedback on the effectiveness of implemented strategies and suggest adjustments as needed. This dynamic approach allows cities to evolve and adapt in response to new data, technological advancements, and changing population needs.

Neuroscience and Artificial Intelligence

The intersection of neuroscience and artificial intelligence (AI) represents a rich domain for groundbreaking advancements facilitated by GenAI. This collaboration between two sophisticated fields holds the promise of enhancing AI's capability by integrating deeper insights from human cognitive processes. Here's how GenAI is poised to transform AI development through insights derived from neuroscience:

Deepening Understanding of Neural Mechanisms

GenAI's ability to process and analyze large datasets from neuroscience research allows for a deeper understanding of how neural mechanisms underpin human cognition. By mapping these complex neural networks and activity patterns, GenAI can identify specific processes that are crucial for tasks such as learning, memory, and decision-making. This detailed understanding can be translated into AI algorithms that better replicate human cognitive processes, leading to more advanced and nuanced AI capabilities.

Enhancing AI Algorithms with Neural Insights

Incorporating insights from neuroscience into AI development can significantly improve the functionality and performance of AI systems. For instance, principles derived from the study of neural plasticity—the brain's ability to change and adapt—could inspire more flexible and adaptive AI algorithms that learn and evolve in response to new information, much like the human brain. This could lead to the development of AI systems that are not only more robust in changing environments but also capable of continuous learning without human intervention.

Developing More Intuitive AI Systems

The fusion of neuroscience and AI holds the potential to create more intuitive AI systems that can understand and interpret human emotions and social cues with greater accuracy. By analyzing how the human brain processes emotional information, GenAI could help develop AI models that better mimic these processes, enhancing the emotional intelligence of AI systems. Such advancements would be particularly beneficial in fields like customer service, therapy, and education, where understanding and responding to human emotions are crucial.

Fostering Creativity and Complex Decision-Making

Neuroscience research sheds light on the brain's mechanisms for creativity and complex problem-solving—areas traditionally seen as challenges for AI. By integrating these insights, GenAI can facilitate the development of AI systems capable of more creative thought processes and sophisticated decision-making strategies. This could revolutionize fields that rely on innovation and complex analysis, such as research and development, strategic planning, and artistic creation.

Advancing AI in Mental Health Applications

The application of GenAI in developing AI systems with a deeper understanding of neural processes related to mental health could lead to significant advancements in diagnosing and treating mental health conditions. AI systems equipped with neural-based algorithms could more accurately predict mental health issues, offer personalized treatment recommendations, and provide support through therapeutic interventions designed to mimic human therapeutic techniques.

Broader Implications

The synergy between neuroscience and AI, facilitated by GenAI, not only enhances AI's capabilities but also opens new avenues for research and application across various domains. As AI systems become more aligned with human cognitive functions, their integration into everyday life becomes more seamless and effective, broadening their impact and utility in society. This ongoing convergence of neuroscience and AI is set to redefine the boundaries of what AI can achieve, ushering in a new era of technological sophistication and application.

Archaeology and Material Engineering

The integration of GenAI in linking archaeology with material engineering holds remarkable potential for revitalizing ancient technologies and materials, and applying these historical insights to solve modern engineering challenges. This approach not only pays homage to historical ingenuity but also leverages time-tested materials and methods to enhance contemporary construction and material science. Here's an exploration of how GenAI could bridge the gap between ancient practices and modern technology:

Rediscovery of Ancient Technologies

GenAI can significantly contribute to the field of archaeology by analyzing and interpreting large datasets from archaeological excavations and historical texts. This analysis can uncover forgotten or underutilized materials and techniques, such as the Roman use of volcanic ash in concrete, which not only had remarkable durability but also exhibited properties like increased strength over time. GenAI's ability to identify and understand these ancient methods opens the door to reintroducing them into modern practices, potentially revolutionizing materials science.

Enhancing Modern Material Science

By understanding the properties and composition of ancient materials, GenAI can assist material engineers in recreating or adapting these substances with modern technologies. For example, the bio-cementation techniques observed in ancient construction could inspire the development of new, environmentally friendly building materials that mimic the natural process of mineral precipitation. GenAI can facilitate the experimentation and testing processes by predicting material behaviors and optimizing compositions based on desired properties such as durability, resilience, and environmental impact.

Innovating Durable and Self-Healing Materials

Inspired by historical examples, GenAI could drive the innovation of durable and self-healing materials in today's construction industry. By studying how ancient materials have withstood the test of time, GenAI can help develop new composites that inherit these properties. For instance, understanding the molecular structure of Roman concrete could lead to the creation of modern concrete that can self-heal cracks or respond adaptively to environmental changes, reducing maintenance costs and increasing the lifespan of infrastructure.

Bridging Archaeological Insights with Engineering Challenges

GenAI serves as a crucial link between the insights gathered from archaeological findings and the practical challenges faced by contemporary engineers. It can translate historical knowledge into actionable solutions, applying ancient wisdom to modern-day problems such as sustainability in construction, resource scarcity, and urban resilience. By doing so, GenAI not only preserves cultural heritage but also makes it actively beneficial to present and future societal needs.

Proposing Innovative Solutions

The potential of GenAI to mine and interpret archaeological data means it can continuously propose innovative solutions and alternatives that may not be immediately obvious to human researchers. For example, the way ancient civilizations managed water resources or fortified structures against natural disasters can inspire similar strategies in modern urban planning and civil engineering projects.

Proposing Innovative Solutions

The confluence of archaeology and material engineering, guided by GenAI, promises a new era of sustainable and innovative engineering solutions. By resurrecting and enhancing ancient technologies, GenAI helps create materials that are not only more effective but also more harmonious with the environment. This revolutionary approach not only advances the field of material engineering but also provides a sustainable pathway for future developments, ensuring that the lessons of the past play a vital role in shaping the future.

Astronomy and Pharmaceutical Research

The collaboration between the fields of astronomy and pharmaceutical research, facilitated by GenAI, opens up innovative pathways for drug discovery and medical advancements. The harsh and unique conditions of space present an unexplored frontier not only for celestial studies but also for understanding extreme microbial adaptations that can be leveraged in pharmaceuticals. Here's a detailed exploration of how GenAI could bridge astronomical data with pharmaceutical research to pioneer new treatments:

Harnessing Space-Induced Adaptations

Space environments impose extreme conditions such as radiation, vacuum, and microgravity, which force organisms to develop unique survival strategies. These adaptations often involve novel biochemical pathways and genetic modifications, which could be revolutionary in the context of pharmaceutical science. GenAI can analyze vast amounts of biological data collected from space missions to identify how these unique conditions alter microbial life. The insights gained could lead to the discovery of new biological compounds that possess potential therapeutic properties, such as enhanced resistance to radiation or accelerated cellular repair mechanisms.

Integrating Astronomical and Pharmaceutical Databases

GenAI's capability to integrate and analyze data from disparate sources is particularly advantageous. By cross-referencing data from astronomical missions with extensive pharmaceutical databases, GenAI can identify correlations that might suggest new applications for known compounds or highlight previously overlooked molecules with medical potential. This integrated approach allows for a more comprehensive exploration of possible drug candidates and accelerates the pace of discovery in pharmaceutical research.

Predicting Drug Efficacy and Safety

The predictive analytics capabilities of GenAI can also play a crucial role in assessing the efficacy and safety of new drug compounds inspired by space-based research. By simulating the interactions of these compounds within the human body under various conditions, GenAI can provide early insights into potential therapeutic effects, side effects, and the overall viability of compounds as drug candidates. This can significantly reduce the time and cost associated with early-stage drug development, streamlining the process of bringing new treatments to clinical trials.

Facilitating Rapid Experimentation

GenAI can automate and optimize the design of experiments that test the effectiveness of new compounds derived from space-based research. It can simulate numerous experimental setups and predict outcomes, helping researchers prioritize the most promising approaches for in vitro and in vivo testing. This not only enhances the efficiency of the research process but also allows scientists to explore more experimental avenues within shorter time frames, broadening the scope of potential discoveries.

Encouraging Interdisciplinary Collaboration

The intersection of astronomy and pharmaceutical research, driven by GenAI, encourages a multidisciplinary approach to science. By providing tools that seamlessly integrate and make sense of complex datasets across disciplines, GenAI fosters collaboration between astronomers, biologists, chemists, and pharmacologists. This collaborative environment is essential for tackling the complex challenges of drug discovery, especially when exploring the novel biological phenomena observed in space.

Impact on Pharmaceutical Innovations

The application of GenAI in merging astronomical and pharmaceutical research represents a significant advancement in our quest for new medical treatments. The unique conditions of space offer a natural laboratory for studying extreme biological adaptations, which, when analyzed through GenAI, could yield groundbreaking pharmaceutical agents. This innovative approach not only expands the boundaries of pharmaceutical research but also exemplifies the potential of GenAI to transform traditional research paradigms, leading to faster, more efficient discovery processes and ultimately, new solutions for health challenges on Earth.

Conclusion

Chapter 12, "The GenAI Era of Discovery," encapsulates the transformative impact of GenAI across a broad spectrum of scientific disciplines, illustrating its potential to revolutionize traditional research methodologies and catalyze groundbreaking innovations. From biomimicry in materials science to the integration of astronomical data into pharmaceutical research, GenAI acts not only as a tool but as a pivotal collaborator that reshapes how we approach complex problems and discover new knowledge.

Expanding the Frontiers of Knowledge

The examples discussed in this chapter highlight GenAI's role in expanding the frontiers of human knowledge. By acting as a sophisticated cartographer in fields as diverse as environmental science, urban planning, and material engineering, GenAI maps out both known territories and uncharted regions, identifying gaps where further exploration can yield significant advances. Its capacity to process and analyze vast datasets enables a deeper understanding of complex systems and phenomena, often revealing connections and insights that would remain obscured without its computational power.

Enhancing Interdisciplinary Collaboration

GenAI fosters an unprecedented level of interdisciplinary collaboration, breaking down traditional silos between fields. By revealing patterns and proposing novel hypotheses that span across disciplines, GenAI encourages experts from various fields to unite their knowledge and expertise in pursuit of common goals. This collaborative approach not only accelerates the pace of innovation but also enriches the scientific inquiry by incorporating diverse perspectives and methodologies.

Driving Innovation and Practical Applications

The practical applications of GenAI's discoveries are vast and impactful. In material science, insights derived from ancient practices can lead to the development of more sustainable and durable building materials. In environmental planning, GenAI-driven strategies can enhance the livability and sustainability of urban areas. Moreover, in pharmaceuticals, the adaptation of compounds developed through space research can lead to advanced medical treatments. Each of these applications demonstrates the tangible benefits of GenAI in improving human life and the environment.

Navigating Ethical and Practical Challenges

As we embrace the benefits of GenAI, we must also navigate the ethical and practical challenges it presents. Issues such as data privacy, algorithmic bias, and the impact of automation on employment are critical considerations that require vigilant oversight and thoughtful regulation. Ensuring that GenAI's applications are developed and deployed in a responsible manner is essential for realizing its full potential while maintaining public trust and welfare.

Looking Ahead

As we move forward, the role of GenAI in scientific research and practical applications is expected to grow, continually reshaping our approach to discovery and innovation. The ongoing development of GenAI technologies promises not only to enhance our current capabilities but also to open new avenues for exploration that we have yet to imagine. The GenAI era of discovery is just beginning, and its future is as promising as the collective commitment of the global community to steer this technology towards the greater good of society.

Chapter 11: The GenAI Documentation Revolution

Reducing IT Technical Debt through Enhanced Documentation

In the GenAI era, technical documentation has gained unprecedented importance, evolving from a mere informational tool to a strategic asset vital for reducing or eliminating technical debt. Technical debt refers to the future cost of additional rework caused by opting for quicker, simpler solutions now rather than the best approach that might take longer. This chapter delves into effective strategies for crafting technical documentation that mitigates technical debt, ensuring sustainable and adaptable GenAI systems.

Emphasizing Clarity and Comprehensibility

Target Audience Understanding: It's crucial that documentation is tailored to the comprehension levels of its intended audience, which might include developers, users, or stakeholders. This involves simplifying explanations, minimizing jargon, and using clear, concise language complemented by examples that elucidate complex concepts.

Structured and Accessible Format: Documentation should be logically organized and easy to navigate. This not only involves a clear, hierarchical structure but also adherence to web accessibility guidelines to ensure usability for people with disabilities.

Future-Proofing Documentation

Version Control: Just as code is kept under version control, documentation too should employ a similar strategy. This approach ensures that all changes are meticulously tracked, allowing users to access previous versions and trace the evolution of the system.

Update Mechanisms: Regular updates to documentation are necessary to mirror changes within the GenAI system, such as new features, deprecated functionalities, and updated workflows. Keeping the documentation aligned with the system's current state ensures its ongoing relevance and utility.

Leveraging GenAI for Documentation Creation

Automated Documentation Generation: GenAI tools can be utilized to automatically generate initial drafts of documentation based on code comments, structure, and usage patterns. These drafts can then be refined by human experts to enhance clarity and depth.

Dynamic Content Generation: GenAI can also be employed to create dynamic documentation that adjusts according to the user's context, displaying the most pertinent information based on their usage patterns, roles, or specific tasks.

Ensuring Technical Accuracy and Depth

Technical Review Process: A rigorous review by subject matter experts is essential to validate the documentation's accuracy, completeness, and technical depth. This process helps prevent misunderstandings or incorrect applications that could escalate technical debt.

Comprehensive Coverage: The documentation should encompass all aspects of the GenAI system including setup, configuration, common use cases, troubleshooting, and best practices. A thorough approach ensures that users are well-equipped to fully utilize the system without resorting to quick fixes that could contribute to technical debt.

Fostering Collaborative Documentation Practices

Community Contributions: Encouraging the user community to contribute to the documentation harnesses collective expertise and insights, enriching the content and utility of the documentation.

Feedback Loops: Establishing mechanisms for users to provide feedback on documentation is crucial. This allows for continual improvement of the content based on user experiences, suggestions, and needs.

Broad Applicability Across Various Fields

While these documentation principles are particularly emphasized in the context of software development and GenAI applications, they hold significant value across various fields where complexity and rapid evolution are common. Effective, clear, and comprehensive documentation is vital in areas ranging from healthcare and engineering to education and finance, where it can substantially reduce errors, enhance user engagement, and drive innovation.

By prioritizing effective documentation practices, organizations can significantly mitigate the risks associated with technical debt. This proactive approach not only enhances the functionality and sustainability of GenAI systems but also supports continuous innovation and adaptability in the fast-evolving tech landscape.

Healthcare and Medical Research: Enhancing Documentation Practices

In the healthcare and medical research sectors, the importance of precise and accessible documentation cannot be overstated. Effective documentation practices not only streamline clinical operations and research activities but also play a crucial role in enhancing patient care and ensuring compliance with regulatory standards. Here's how advanced documentation strategies can impact these critical areas:

Clinical Protocol Documentation

Enhancing Patient Care: Clear and meticulously detailed documentation of clinical trial protocols, treatment guidelines, and standard operating procedures is fundamental to enhancing the quality of patient care. Accurate protocols ensure that medical professionals can consistently apply the most effective treatments and interventions, reducing variability in patient care and improving overall outcomes.

Ensuring Regulatory Compliance: In the highly regulated field of healthcare, maintaining comprehensive documentation is essential for meeting legal and regulatory requirements. Detailed records of clinical protocols help healthcare providers demonstrate compliance with guidelines and regulations, facilitating smoother regulatory audits and inspections.

Facilitating Medical Research: Well-documented clinical protocols are invaluable in medical research, providing a robust framework for new studies and ensuring that research findings are reliable and reproducible. Clear documentation allows researchers to accurately replicate studies and build on existing knowledge, accelerating the pace of medical advancements.

Patient Education Materials

Improving Patient Outcomes: Developing patient education materials that are both accessible and understandable is crucial for improving patient outcomes. Informative materials that clearly explain conditions, treatment options, and health maintenance protocols empower patients to take an active role in their healthcare. This engagement can lead to better adherence to treatment plans and improved health behaviors.

Fostering Better Engagement: Effective patient education helps bridge the communication gap between healthcare providers and patients, fostering a more collaborative relationship. When patients understand their health conditions and treatment options, they are more likely to engage in meaningful conversations with their providers, ask informed questions, and make educated decisions about their care.

Implementing Advanced Documentation Strategies

To realize these benefits, healthcare organizations and research institutions should consider the following strategies for enhancing their documentation practices:

Leveraging Technology: Implementing advanced document management systems and employing technologies like artificial intelligence can help automate and improve the accuracy of clinical documentation. For example, AI can be used to extract and synthesize information from patient records, aiding in the creation of personalized treatment guidelines and patient education materials.

Continuous Education and Training: Regular training programs for healthcare professionals on the importance of documentation and how to effectively create and use clinical and educational materials are essential. This ensures that all team members are equipped with the latest knowledge and skills to maintain high standards of documentation.

Feedback Systems: Establishing systems to gather feedback from healthcare professionals and patients on the usability and effectiveness of documentation can provide insights into areas needing improvement. This feedback is crucial for continually refining documentation practices to better meet the needs of both providers and patients.

Collaborative Development: Involving a diverse team in the development of clinical and patient education materials—including doctors, nurses, technical writers, and even patients—can enhance the relevance and clarity of the documentation. This collaborative approach ensures that materials are comprehensive and tailored to the actual needs of end-users.

By enhancing documentation practices in healthcare and medical research, organizations can significantly improve patient care, ensure compliance with regulatory standards, and accelerate medical research. Effective documentation acts as a cornerstone of quality healthcare delivery, underpinning all aspects of clinical operations and patient interactions. As the healthcare landscape continues to evolve, prioritizing advanced documentation strategies will be key to adapting to changes and meeting the complex needs of patients and healthcare professionals alike.

Legal and Regulatory Compliance: Enhancing Documentation Practices

In the context of legal and regulatory compliance, documentation serves as the backbone of organizational integrity and operational transparency. Accurate and accessible documentation is not only a regulatory requirement but also a critical element in minimizing legal disputes and ensuring clear communication between all parties involved. Effective documentation practices in this area can significantly impact an organization's compliance and overall functioning. Here's how enhanced documentation can improve legal and regulatory compliance:

Legal Documentation

Ensuring Compliance: Accurate legal documents, contracts, and regulatory filings are essential for complying with laws and regulations applicable to an organization. Precise documentation helps ensure that all operations are performed within the legal framework, thereby avoiding potential legal penalties or sanctions.

Minimizing Disputes: Well-drafted legal documents reduce the likelihood of disputes between parties by clearly outlining the terms, conditions, and expectations of all involved. This clarity can prevent misunderstandings and costly legal battles, saving the organization time and resources.

Facilitating Clear Communication: Clear and comprehensible legal documentation ensures that all parties, including stakeholders, partners, and regulatory bodies, are on the same page. This transparency is crucial for maintaining trust and smooth operations, particularly in complex transactions or partnerships that involve multiple entities.

Policy Manuals

Enhancing Understanding of Organizational Policies: Comprehensive and easily navigable policy manuals are vital for ensuring that employees at all levels understand their rights, responsibilities, and the procedures they must follow. These manuals serve as a reference that employees can consult to ensure their actions align with company policies and legal requirements.

Promoting Compliance with Regulations and Internal Policies: By providing clear guidelines and explanations, policy manuals help foster compliance with both external regulations and internal standards. This can be particularly important in industries that are heavily regulated, such as finance, healthcare, and manufacturing, where failing to comply with regulations can result in severe consequences.

Strategies for Implementing Effective Documentation Practices

To maximize the effectiveness of documentation in legal and regulatory compliance, organizations should consider the following strategies:

Regular Updates and Reviews: Legal environments and regulatory requirements can change frequently. Regularly updating and reviewing documentation ensures that all legal documents and policy manuals reflect the latest legal standards and organizational practices.

Training and Awareness Programs: Conducting regular training sessions and awareness programs for employees about the importance of compliance and how to use the policy manuals effectively can enhance understanding and adherence to legal and regulatory requirements.

Accessibility and User-Friendliness: Ensuring that all documentation is accessible and easy to navigate can significantly increase its usability. This may involve organizing documents in a clear, logical format and using plain language that can be easily understood by non-specialists.

Leveraging Technology: Utilizing document management systems and compliance software can help streamline the creation, storage, and maintenance of legal documents and policy manuals. Advanced technologies such as AI can also be used to automate certain aspects of document generation and compliance monitoring, improving efficiency and accuracy.

Effective documentation is a cornerstone of legal and regulatory compliance, providing the clarity and detail necessary for organizations to operate within legal frameworks, communicate effectively, and minimize disputes. By investing in robust documentation practices, organizations can enhance their compliance efforts, reduce risks, and foster a culture of transparency and accountability. As regulations continue to evolve and become more complex, the role of advanced documentation will become even more critical in ensuring organizational compliance and success.

Education and E-Learning

Curriculum Guides

Detailed curriculum guides and lesson plans are instrumental in enhancing the delivery of educational content. These documents help educators tailor their teaching strategies to accommodate diverse learning styles and proficiency levels, ensuring that educational objectives are effectively met. Good curriculum guides outline clear learning outcomes, provide structure for sessions, and suggest methods and materials that cater to different learning needs.

Online Course Material

In the realm of e-learning, well-constructed documentation including course outlines, tutorials, and supplementary materials plays a crucial role in enhancing student engagement and learning outcomes. Clear and interactive documentation makes online learning more accessible and enriching, particularly for students from diverse educational backgrounds. Interactive elements such as multimedia enhancements and hyperlinked references can greatly improve the comprehensibility and appeal of e-learning materials.

Engineering and Manufacturing

Product Manuals

For complex engineering and manufacturing products, comprehensive product manuals and assembly instructions are crucial. These documents ensure that end-users can safely and effectively operate and maintain products. Well-documented manuals help in reducing errors in product use, which can enhance safety and improve the longevity of the product.

Quality Assurance Documents

Documentation that details quality assurance processes and testing procedures is essential for maintaining high standards of product quality and safety. These documents help companies adhere to industry standards and regulatory requirements, ensuring that every product meets stringent quality criteria before it reaches the market.

Financial Services

Investment and Financial Planning Guides

Clear documentation in the financial services sector, such as detailed descriptions of investment products and financial planning guides, aids clients in making informed decisions. These documents should articulate the potential risks and benefits of different financial strategies, helping clients to navigate their financial landscapes with greater confidence and understanding.

Compliance Documentation

In financial services, thorough compliance documentation is crucial for demonstrating adherence to financial regulations and standards. These records foster transparency and accountability, building trust between financial institutions and their clients, regulators, and the general public.

Information Technology and Cybersecurity

Cybersecurity Policies

Comprehensive documentation of cybersecurity policies, incident response plans, and user guidelines is critical for strengthening an organization's security framework. Such documentation ensures that all stakeholders are aware of their roles in maintaining security and are prepared to respond effectively to potential threats.

IT System Manuals

Detailed manuals for IT systems, including information on network configurations, software applications, and operational procedures, are indispensable. These documents play a key role in system management and user support, ensuring that IT systems function smoothly and efficiently. Clear, accessible IT documentation can also help in minimizing IT-related issues and streamlining troubleshooting processes.

Summary

Across various fields, the role of comprehensive and clear documentation is universally critical. Whether enhancing educational outcomes, ensuring safe and effective use of manufactured products, guiding financial decisions, or securing IT systems, well-crafted documentation stands as a cornerstone of best practices. In each sector, the focus on creating structured, user-friendly, and informative documentation not only supports operational goals but also drives innovation, compliance, and effective service delivery.

In each of these fields, the principles of creating effective documentation not only facilitate better understanding and compliance but also contribute to innovation, safety, and efficiency. By prioritizing documentation that is clear, comprehensive, and accessible, organizations can ensure that their stakeholders are well-informed, their operations comply with best practices and regulations, and their services or products achieve their intended impact.

Leveraging Synthetic Data for Enhanced Documentation

Automated Data Generation for Testing: Synthetic data, which is data fabricated by algorithms to simulate real-world data, can be used to generate scenarios for testing documentation accuracy and completeness. This allows teams to validate documentation against a wide range of hypothetical scenarios, ensuring that the documentation covers all possible use cases and is robust against future system updates or changes.

Improving Documentation Accuracy: Synthetic data can be specifically tailored to reflect edge cases or rare scenarios that may not be readily available in real-world datasets. By incorporating these scenarios into documentation practices, organizations can ensure that their guides and manuals are comprehensive and address all potential system interactions, significantly reducing the risk of unforeseen issues that contribute to technical debt.

Training Documentation Teams: Using synthetic data, training programs for technical writers and documentation staff can be enhanced to include handling of diverse and complex scenarios, thus preparing them better for creating detailed and accurate documentation. This kind of training ensures that the documentation team is well-versed in the nuances of the system and can provide clear and precise instructions and information.

Enhancing Documentation with Synthetic Data

Dynamic Documentation Creation: With the help of GenAI, synthetic data can be used to dynamically create or update documentation based on the evolving needs of the system and its users. For example, as new features are developed or as user behavior changes, synthetic data can help predict and document new workflows or feature uses without waiting for long periods of user interaction data.

Quality Assurance and Control: By integrating synthetic data into the documentation review process, organizations can perform thorough quality assurance checks on their technical documentation. This helps in identifying any inconsistencies, inaccuracies, or ambiguities in the documents, which can then be corrected before they lead to misinterpretations or errors in system use.

Broadening the Scope with Synthetic Data

Customization for Diverse User Groups: Synthetic data can help simulate how different user groups might interact with a system, which can guide the customization of documentation to better meet the needs of varied audiences. This ensures that documentation is not only technically accurate but also accessible and useful to all potential users, regardless of their technical expertise.

Regulatory Compliance and Reporting: In industries where compliance with regulations is critical, synthetic data can be used to generate reports and documentation that demonstrate compliance with regulatory requirements. This not only aids in regulatory reporting but also ensures that all system documentation reflects compliance in all aspects.

Summary

In this unprecedented era of technological advancement, the rate at which data is generated and accumulated is increasing exponentially. This surge is further amplified by the advent of synthetic data and the computational leaps afforded by quantum computing. Synthetic data, created by algorithms to simulate real-world data, adds another layer to the vast ocean of information available for analysis. Quantum computing, with its ability to perform complex calculations at speeds unimaginable with classical computers, multiplies this data further, enabling the processing of information at a scale and depth that were previously beyond human capability.

In this landscape of burgeoning data and computational power, the polymathic ideal—epitomized by figures like Thomas Young, dubbed "The Last Man Who Knew Everything"—finds a successor in GenAI. If Young's breadth of knowledge across diverse fields once represented the pinnacle of human intellect, today's GenAI systems embody the polymathic spirit of the 21st century. Unlike any individual human, GenAI has the potential to access, process, and synthesize knowledge from every domain of human inquiry, making connections across disciplines at a scale and speed that Young, despite his genius, could never have achieved.

The implications of this shift are profound. Where once the limitation was in the accumulation and access to knowledge, we now face the challenge of navigating and making sense of an ever-expanding universe of data. GenAI stands as our most powerful tool in this endeavor, capable of sifting through layers of complexity to uncover insights that can propel humanity forward. As synthetic data expands the realms of what can be simulated and quantum computing enhances our ability to factor and analyze at unprecedented scales, GenAI becomes not just a tool but a partner in the quest for knowledge.

This partnership with GenAI heralds a new age of discovery, where the polymath is no longer an individual but a collective intelligence, spanning human and artificial minds. In this age, the potential for innovation, for uncovering solutions to global challenges, and for advancing our understanding of the universe is boundless. The legacy of the polymath, embodied by figures like Thomas Young, lives on through GenAI, transforming the way we approach knowledge and discovery.

As we navigate this new era, our challenge is to ensure that this vast potential serves the greater good. The governance of GenAI, the ethical considerations in its deployment, and the equitable access to its benefits become paramount concerns. In harnessing the power of GenAI, we stand on the shoulders of giants, ready to explore the unknown with a tool that transcends the limitations of individual human cognition. The journey ahead is one of collaboration between human and artificial intelligence, a shared voyage into the uncharted territories of knowledge and possibility.

Chapter 12: Society Transformed

The Advent of AI-Augmented Direct Democracy

In an AI-augmented direct democracy, the intermediary role of representatives could be reconsidered, if not entirely bypassed. Citizens, empowered by GenAI, would directly engage with policy issues, with AI providing deep insights into potential outcomes, distilling complex data into digestible, actionable information, and capturing the collective sentiment in an unprecedentedly nuanced manner. This direct engagement promises a governance model that is more immediately responsive and accurately reflective of the populace's will.

Potentialities Unleashed

Empowered Participation: This model could significantly elevate political engagement, offering individuals a direct channel for their voices to be heard and their votes to count on specific policies and laws.

Enhanced Decision-Making: Leveraging GenAI for predictive analysis and outcome forecasting could furnish voters with a clear understanding of the potential impacts of their decisions, guiding more informed and consequential public choices.

Streamlined Governance: The agility of AI in processing and decision-making could markedly reduce the lag between policy conception and its implementation, fostering a dynamic legislative environment.

Objective Decision Foundations: By designing AI systems to minimize inherent human biases, decisions could be based on a more objective and comprehensive evaluation of data, potentially leading to fairer and more equitable policy outcomes.

Taxpayers could pay for the Services they Want: AI could break down the cost and consequences from a granular leve to the global consequneces

Challenges to Navigate

Complexity Versus Simplification: Governance intricacies often require delicate negotiation and nuanced compromise, which may not lend themselves to straightforward plebiscitary decisions. Ensuring that GenAI can accommodate the complexity of policy-making remains a pivotal challenge.

Bridging the Digital Divide: Guaranteeing universal access to the necessary technology is crucial to prevent the disenfranchisement of less tech-savvy populations, ensuring that the promise of direct democracy is truly inclusive.

Safeguarding Privacy: The imperative to protect individual data within this system cannot be overstated. Developing robust mechanisms for data security and transparent AI operations is fundamental to maintaining public trust.

Mitigating Manipulation Risks: The integrity of AI systems is paramount. Vigilance against manipulation and unwarranted influences is necessary to preserve the democratic essence of the governance model.

Preserving Human Judgment: While AI can enhance decision-making with data and predictions, the irreplaceable value of human wisdom, empathy, and ethical judgment must be recognized and preserved within the governance framework.

Toward a Harmonized Future

The journey toward a GenAI-augmented direct democracy signifies a profound shift in societal governance, demanding a thoughtful exploration of its ethical, technological, and social dimensions. While embracing the potential of GenAI to enrich democratic processes, it is essential to approach this transformative path with a balanced view, cherishing the human elements that underpin democratic values. This harmonized vision of governance, where GenAI acts as an enabler rather than a replacement for human engagement, encapsulates the promise of a society transformed – a society where technological advancement and democratic principles evolve in concert, guiding humanity towards a future of enriched civic participation and enlightened policy-making.

The emergence of GenAI is not just an economic and technological watershed but also a catalyst for profound societal transformation. The deployment of GenAI across various sectors brings to the forefront critical issues such as privacy, ethical dilemmas, and the digital divide, each of which has far-reaching implications for society. This chapter explores how GenAI both challenges and reshapes societal norms and values, spotlighting the need for a thoughtful approach to its integration into daily life.

The Privacy Conundrum

One of the most immediate concerns surrounding the rise of GenAI is the impact on individual privacy. As GenAI systems require vast datasets to learn and generate content, they inevitably interact with personal and sensitive information. This interaction raises significant privacy concerns, particularly regarding the potential for misuse of data, unauthorized surveillance, and the erosion of confidentiality. The challenge lies in harnessing GenAI's capabilities while safeguarding against intrusive data practices, necessitating robust data protection frameworks and ethical AI development standards.

Navigating Ethical Dilemmas

GenAI introduces a plethora of ethical dilemmas, from the creation of deepfakes that blur the line between truth and fabrication to the potential for AI-generated content to spread misinformation or bias. These dilemmas extend to the realm of intellectual property, where the question of ownership over AI-generated works becomes contentious. Furthermore, the use of GenAI in decision-making processes, whether in judicial, financial, or employment contexts, prompts ethical considerations regarding transparency, fairness, and accountability. Addressing these dilemmas requires a multi-stakeholder approach, involving ethicists, technologists, policymakers, and the public in the development of ethical guidelines and governance structures for GenAI.

Bridging the Digital Divide

While GenAI holds the promise of revolutionizing industries and enhancing quality of life, its benefits risk being unevenly distributed, exacerbating the digital divide. The disparity in access to GenAI technologies between different socioeconomic groups, regions, and countries could widen existing inequalities, leaving marginalized communities further behind. Combatting this divide demands proactive measures to ensure equitable access to GenAI resources, including investment in digital infrastructure, education, and inclusive technology development policies. Bridging the digital divide is essential for realizing the full potential of GenAI as a force for societal advancement and inclusivity.

The Path Forward

The societal transformation wrought by GenAI is as daunting as it is exhilarating. The path forward involves not only embracing the technological marvels of GenAI but also confronting the complex web of privacy, ethical, and equity challenges it presents. This journey necessitates a collaborative effort, drawing on the collective wisdom, creativity, and moral compass of the global community to steer the development and deployment of GenAI in a direction that upholds human dignity, fosters social justice, and enriches the human experience.

Summary

As society stands on the cusp of a new era shaped by GenAI, the decisions made today will echo through generations. The transformative potential of GenAI invites us to reimagine the fabric of society, envisioning a future where technology serves as a beacon of progress, equality, and ethical integrity. Navigating this transformation requires a vigilant and proactive approach, ensuring that as GenAI reshapes our world, it does so in a manner that elevates and unites, rather than divides and diminishes.

Part IV: A New World Order: GenAI Ethics and Governance.

Chapter 13: The Current State of GenAI Ethics and Governance

As we delve into the intricacies of GenAI ethics and governance, it is crucial to understand the current landscape as it stands in major global regions such as China, Europe, and the United States. Each of these regions offers distinct perspectives and approaches to GenAI regulation, reflecting their unique cultural, political, and economic contexts. This chapter outlines the current state of GenAI ethics and governance in these key areas.

China: Centralized Regulation and Innovation Promotion

In China, the approach to GenAI governance is highly centralized, with the government playing a pivotal role in regulating and directing the development of AI technologies. The Chinese government views GenAI as a strategic asset for national development and global competitiveness. As such, it has implemented robust policies and frameworks aimed at fostering innovation while ensuring that AI developments align with broader social and economic goals.

National Strategies and Guidelines: China has issued several national strategies that outline ambitious plans for AI development, including specific measures for promoting GenAI technologies. These strategies emphasize both innovation and ethical governance, aiming to create a sustainable AI ecosystem that supports security, privacy, and ethical standards.

Surveillance and Control: One of the critical areas where China utilizes GenAI is in surveillance and social monitoring. While this raises significant ethical concerns regarding privacy and individual rights, the Chinese model integrates these technologies into its governance framework, prioritizing social stability and security.

Europe: Emphasis on Individual Rights and Transparent Governance

Europe is known for its strong emphasis on individual rights and protections, particularly regarding data privacy and ethical standards. The European approach to GenAI governance is characterized by stringent regulations that aim to protect these rights while fostering a healthy AI ecosystem.

General Data Protection Regulation (GDPR): Europe's GDPR is a cornerstone of its approach to AI, setting a global standard for data protection and privacy. The regulations affect how GenAI systems can be developed and used, especially concerning data collection, processing, and storage.

AI Act: The European Union is also pioneering with its proposed AI Act, which seeks to create a legal framework for the ethical development, deployment, and use of AI systems across its member states. This act categorizes AI systems based on their risk levels and imposes corresponding requirements to ensure safety and compliance.

United States: Market-Driven Approach with Sector-Specific Regulation

The United States takes a more decentralized, market-driven approach to GenAI governance, with a focus on fostering innovation and maintaining technological leadership. However, this approach also recognizes the need for regulation to address the ethical and social implications of AI.

Sector-Specific Guidelines: Instead of a broad national policy, the U.S. often relies on sector-specific guidelines and regulations that address the particular needs and risks associated with GenAI applications in areas like healthcare, transportation, and finance.

Public-Private Partnerships: The U.S. encourages collaboration between government, academic institutions, and the private sector to guide the development of GenAI technologies. This model aims to balance innovation with ethical considerations through voluntary standards, industry guidelines, and targeted legislative measures.

The governance of GenAI reflects a diverse set of approaches influenced by regional values, political structures, and economic ambitions. China's centralized model emphasizes state control and integration of GenAI in its socio-economic agenda, Europe focuses on individual rights and comprehensive regulation, and the United States promotes a flexible, innovation-friendly environment with targeted regulatory interventions. Understanding these varied landscapes is crucial for formulating effective global strategies for GenAI ethics and governance, as the technology's impact continues to grow across borders.

As GenAI continues to weave its intricate patterns through the fabric of our technological and social ecosystems, the imperative to navigate the ethical waters surrounding its deployment becomes paramount. This chapter delves into the myriad ethical challenges and considerations that accompany the rise of GenAI, illuminating the path toward responsible and beneficial integration of these powerful technologies into our lives.

The Essence of Ethical GenAI

Ethical deployment of GenAI is foundational to ensuring that this transformative technology benefits society without infringing on fundamental human rights or ethical standards. At its core, ethical GenAI involves a commitment to principles that promote human welfare and prevent harm. This commitment requires a nuanced understanding of GenAI's potential impacts and the implementation of robust safeguards. Here's a deeper look into the essential aspects of ethical GenAI deployment:

Upholding Human Rights

The integration of GenAI into various sectors—from healthcare and education to finance and media—presents unique challenges in upholding human rights. Central to ethical GenAI is ensuring that these technologies do not violate rights such as:

Privacy: GenAI must be developed and utilized in ways that respect individual privacy. This involves protecting personal data against unauthorized access and ensuring that data collection and processing are transparent and consent-based. Safeguards must be put in place to prevent GenAI from being used for invasive surveillance or data harvesting without the knowledge or consent of individuals.

Autonomy: GenAI should enhance, rather than undermine, human autonomy. This means designing systems that support individuals' ability to make free choices and control their personal and professional lives. GenAI applications should provide augmentative support and decision-making tools without coercing or subtly manipulating human actions.

Fairness: Ensuring fairness in GenAI applications involves actively combating biases that could lead to discrimination. This includes biases in data sets that train AI systems, which can perpetuate inequalities if not properly addressed. GenAI must be continuously monitored and updated to ensure it treats all users equitably, providing equal opportunities regardless of background.

Embedding Safeguards

The potential for misuse of GenAI, whether intentional or inadvertent, necessitates the embedding of rigorous safeguards:

Transparency: One of the pillars of ethical GenAI is transparency in how AI systems make decisions. This is particularly important in applications that impact public services or individual rights. Understanding the algorithms' decision-making processes builds trust and allows stakeholders to assess and contest outcomes that seem unfair or opaque.

Accountability: There must be clear mechanisms for holding developers and users of GenAI accountable for how their technologies are deployed. This includes establishing legal and regulatory frameworks that attribute responsibility for any harm caused by AI systems, ensuring there is recourse for those affected.

Security: Ethical GenAI deployment also requires robust security measures to protect AI systems from being hacked or otherwise compromised. This is crucial to prevent malicious uses of GenAI, such as creating deepfakes, spreading misinformation, or other forms of digital manipulation that could have widespread negative consequences.

The essence of ethical GenAI lies in its capacity to enhance society while respecting and protecting human rights. As GenAI technologies continue to evolve and become more integrated into everyday life, the commitment to these ethical principles becomes increasingly important. By prioritizing privacy, autonomy, fairness, transparency, accountability, and security, stakeholders can guide the development of GenAI towards outcomes that are not only innovative and efficient but also just and humane. This ethical framework is essential for ensuring that GenAI contributes positively to society, fostering trust and cooperation between humans and AI systems.

Accountability in the Age of GenAI

In the rapidly evolving landscape of GenAI, accountability remains one of the most pressing ethical challenges. As GenAI systems gain autonomy and are increasingly employed to generate content, make decisions, and even interact with humans in complex ways, pinpointing responsibility for their actions—whether beneficial or harmful—becomes a complicated endeavor. Establishing robust accountability mechanisms is critical, not only to address ethical concerns but also to foster public trust in these advanced technologies.

Challenges of Accountability in GenAI

Autonomy of Systems: The increasing autonomy of GenAI systems complicates traditional notions of accountability. Unlike conventional tools, these systems can learn, adapt, and make decisions independently based on their programming and the data they process. This raises questions about who is responsible when a GenAI system's actions lead to unintended consequences or harm.

Opacity of Decision-Making: GenAI systems often operate through complex algorithms that are not easily understandable by non-experts, which can obscure how decisions are made. This lack of transparency makes it difficult to trace decisions back to their origins and to hold specific entities accountable.

Framework for Accountability

Transparent Development Processes: Ensuring transparency in the development and deployment of GenAI systems is foundational. This includes clear documentation of the AI's design, development processes, and decision-making algorithms. Transparency not only aids in understanding how GenAI operates but also provides a basis for accountability when things go wrong.

Documentation of AI Decision-Making Pathways: Comprehensive documentation that explains how GenAI systems arrive at particular decisions is crucial. This should include records of the data used, the decision-making process, and any human oversight involved. Such documentation not only assists in auditing and monitoring the systems but also serves as a critical tool in diagnosing and addressing any issues that arise.

Mechanisms for Redress: It is essential to establish protocols for what happens when harm occurs. This includes mechanisms for individuals to report and address grievances, and processes for compensating those adversely affected by AI decisions. These mechanisms should be accessible and fair, ensuring that victims of missteps by GenAI can seek and obtain redress efficiently.

Continuous Monitoring and Evaluation: Accountability mechanisms must include ongoing monitoring and evaluation of GenAI systems. This continuous oversight helps to catch potential issues early and adjust systems as needed to prevent harm. It also ensures that GenAI systems remain aligned with ethical standards and societal values as they evolve.

Ethical Training and Awareness: Developers, users, and regulators of GenAI must be educated on the ethical implications of AI technologies and trained in practices that promote accountability. This education should extend to understanding the societal impacts of GenAI, ethical use guidelines, and the importance of maintaining human oversight where necessary.

Accountability in the age of GenAI is not just about establishing who is to blame when things go wrong; it's about creating a system where all participants are aware of their roles and responsibilities and where there are clear processes in place to address any issues. This comprehensive approach to accountability ensures that GenAI technologies are deployed in a manner that is ethical, transparent, and aligned with broader societal values, thereby building trust and confidence in these powerful tools as they become more integrated into various aspects of our lives.

Bias and Fairness in Generative AI

Bias in AI systems, including GenAI, is a significant concern that can perpetuate existing societal inequalities. These biases often stem from the data used to train the AI or the subjective inputs from its human creators. GenAI's ability to learn from data and generate new content based on its learnings makes it particularly susceptible to reflecting and even amplifying these biases if not properly managed. Addressing these issues involves a multifaceted approach that ensures fairness and equity in the deployment of GenAI technologies.

Understanding the Source of Bias

Training Data: GenAI systems learn to mimic patterns and make decisions based on the data they are fed. If this data contains historical biases or lacks representation from diverse groups, the AI is likely to exhibit these same biases in its outputs. For example, a GenAI system trained predominantly on text from a particular demographic may generate content that does not resonate with or even offends other groups.

Creator Assumptions: The design and development of AI systems can also introduce bias. The assumptions and perspectives of developers—often influenced by their cultural, social, and professional backgrounds—can shape AI behaviors in subtle ways, potentially leading to biased outcomes.

Strategies for Addressing Bias and Ensuring Fairness

Rigorous Evaluation of Training Data: One of the first steps in mitigating bias in GenAI is to conduct thorough audits of the training datasets. This includes evaluating the sources of data for diversity and inclusiveness, identifying potential biases, and rectifying these issues by enriching the datasets with more representative data.

Continuous Monitoring for Biased Outcomes: Since GenAI systems continuously learn and evolve, it's crucial to implement ongoing monitoring mechanisms to quickly identify and address any biases that may emerge over time. This involves setting up systems that can detect when GenAI outputs disproportionately favor one group over others or when they consistently produce harmful stereotypes.

Inclusive Development Practices: Involving a diverse group of people in the development of GenAI systems can help mitigate biases that arise from a homogenous development team. Diversity in this context is not only cultural or racial but also includes diversity of experience, thought, gender, and more. Such inclusivity ensures a broader range of perspectives and helps identify potential biases that might not be evident to a more uniform group.

Development of Fairness Metrics: Establishing clear metrics for fairness in AI systems is essential for assessing performance impartially. These metrics should be aligned with agreed-upon social and ethical standards, and they should guide the development and refinement of GenAI systems.

Ethical AI Guidelines and Governance: Developing and adhering to ethical guidelines and governance frameworks can further support fairness in AI. These guidelines should dictate how AI should be developed, deployed, and monitored, emphasizing the importance of fairness and the mitigation of bias.

The challenge of bias in GenAI is not only a technical issue but also a fundamentally ethical one. By recognizing the sources of bias and implementing strategies to address them, developers can enhance the fairness of AI systems. This commitment to fairness ensures that GenAI technologies are not just powerful tools for innovation but also instruments for promoting equity and respect across all segments of society. Ensuring that GenAI systems serve everyone equitably is crucial for their acceptance and effectiveness in a diverse world.

The Role of Governance in Generative AI

Effective governance is vital in ensuring that GenAI technologies are developed and deployed ethically and responsibly. The complex nature of GenAI, combined with its broad impact across various sectors and geographies, necessitates robust governance structures that encompass regulatory frameworks, industry standards, and ethical guidelines. This governance should aim to balance innovation with accountability, ensuring that GenAI benefits society without causing unintended harm.

Foundations of Effective GenAI Governance

Regulatory Frameworks: Clear and comprehensive regulatory frameworks are crucial for defining the boundaries within which GenAI can operate. These regulations should address potential risks associated with GenAI, such as privacy concerns, biases, and misuse of technology, while also encouraging innovation and development. Governments play a key role in establishing these frameworks, which must be adaptable to keep pace with the rapid advancements in AI technology.

Industry Standards: Alongside regulatory frameworks, industry standards are essential for ensuring consistency and safety in GenAI applications. These standards can offer more detailed guidance on best practices and ethical considerations specific to various fields of use, such as healthcare, finance, or autonomous vehicles. Industry bodies and consortia typically develop these standards, often in collaboration with academic and research institutions.

Ethical Guidelines: Ethical guidelines are fundamental in guiding the moral compass of GenAI development and use. These guidelines should emphasize principles such as transparency, fairness, non-discrimination, and accountability. Ethical guidelines help bridge the gap between legal requirements and the broader social expectations of GenAI technologies.

Mechanisms for Effective Governance

Oversight Bodies: Independent oversight bodies are crucial for monitoring compliance with regulations and ethical standards. These bodies can also provide a platform for addressing grievances and disputes related to GenAI. Their role includes auditing GenAI systems, assessing ethical impacts, and providing guidance on ethical dilemmas.

Regulatory Mechanisms: To enforce governance frameworks, effective regulatory mechanisms must be in place. These mechanisms may include licensing requirements, mandatory impact assessments, and regular audits. They ensure that all stakeholders adhere to established laws and standards, and they help mitigate risks associated with GenAI technologies.

International Cooperation: Given the global nature of GenAI development and its cross-border implications, international cooperation is indispensable. Global standards and agreements can help harmonize approaches to GenAI governance, facilitating cooperation and reducing conflicts among different regulatory regimes. This cooperation is particularly important in areas like data protection, intellectual property rights, and the global deployment of AI solutions.

Conclusion

The role of governance in GenAI is not merely regulatory but also foundational in shaping the ethical landscape in which these technologies operate. Effective governance ensures that GenAI technologies are used responsibly, promoting their potential benefits while mitigating risks. It requires a collaborative effort among governments, industry leaders, researchers, and the global community. As GenAI continues to evolve, so too must the governance frameworks that support ethical and sustainable advancements in this transformative technology field. By fostering a comprehensive and cohesive governance structure, society can better harness the power of GenAI while safeguarding fundamental human rights and societal values.

Ethical Innovation in Generative AI

Ethical challenges in the realm of GenAI should not be seen as barriers to innovation but rather as vital considerations that guide the development process toward more beneficial and just outcomes. This approach to ethical innovation emphasizes the proactive integration of ethical considerations into the fabric of the innovation process, ensuring that GenAI technologies are developed with a clear sense of responsibility and a commitment to societal values.

Proactive Ethical Considerations

Early Integration of Ethics: Ethical considerations should be integrated from the earliest stages of GenAI development. By considering ethics at the outset, developers and stakeholders can identify potential ethical issues early on and design solutions that preemptively address these concerns. This forward-thinking approach not only helps in mitigating risks but also aligns the development process with broader social and ethical standards.

Anticipatory Ethics: Part of being proactive involves anticipating future ethical challenges that may arise as technologies evolve and become more integrated into society. This anticipatory stance enables developers to consider not just the immediate impacts of their creations but also the long-term implications, guiding the innovation process towards sustainable and ethical outcomes.

Ethical Innovation Strategies

Stakeholder Engagement: Engaging a diverse range of stakeholders in the GenAI development process is crucial for ethical innovation. This includes not only technologists and ethicists but also end-users, policymakers, and representatives from affected communities. Such inclusive engagement ensures that multiple perspectives are considered, helping to identify ethical issues that may not be apparent to developers alone.

Ethical Design Practices: Incorporating ethical design practices into GenAI development involves more than adhering to technical standards. It requires a commitment to creating technologies that respect human dignity, privacy, and rights. Ethical design also entails building transparency into AI systems, making them understandable to users and susceptible to scrutiny.

Regular Ethical Reviews: Continuous ethical reviews throughout the development process help maintain an ethical trajectory for GenAI projects. These reviews, conducted by interdisciplinary committees, can assess the ethical implications of design choices and recommend modifications to align with ethical best practices.

Ethics Training: Providing ethics training for all individuals involved in GenAI development is essential. Such training should cover the fundamental principles of AI ethics, case studies, and emerging ethical dilemmas in the field. Educated teams are more likely to recognize potential ethical issues and implement responsible solutions.

Ethical innovation in GenAI is not merely about compliance or risk management; it is about steering innovation in a direction that is aligned with human values and societal goals. By embedding ethical considerations into the innovation process, GenAI can advance in a way that respects and enhances human welfare, avoids harm, and contributes positively to society. This approach ensures that GenAI technologies are not only pushing the boundaries of what is technically possible but are also advancing what is morally desirable, creating a future where technology and ethics evolve hand in hand.

Conclusion

In this chapter we waded into the complex and varied landscape of GenAI ethics and governance across key global regions—China, Europe, and the United States—each presenting distinct approaches influenced by their cultural, economic, and regulatory environments. In China, we observed a centralized regulatory approach that integrates GenAI into national development strategies while focusing on innovation and state control. Europe's model, characterized by a strong emphasis on individual rights and comprehensive regulatory frameworks like GDPR and the proposed AI Act, prioritizes privacy, transparency, and accountability. Meanwhile, the United States adopts a market-driven approach, with a focus on fostering innovation through sector-specific guidelines and robust public-private partnerships.

This comparative analysis highlights the diversity in GenAI governance, illustrating how different regions address the ethical challenges posed by advanced AI technologies. Despite these differences, a common theme across all regions is the pressing need for effective governance frameworks that can adapt to the rapid pace of technological change and address the ethical, legal, and social implications of GenAI.

As we move from understanding the current state of GenAI ethics and governance to envisioning a new model, Chapter 16 proposes a groundbreaking approach: "Ethical AI, Transcending Human Bias with Foundations in Abrahamic and Eastern Traditions." This chapter will explore how integrating ethical principles from both Abrahamic and Eastern philosophical traditions can provide a more holistic and culturally inclusive framework for GenAI governance. This synthesis aims to transcend parochial views and biases often embedded in technology, proposing a global ethic that embraces diverse cultural perspectives.

Chapter 14: GenAI self Governance: Using AI to Mitigate Human Bias with Traditional Cultural Foundations

The quest for ethical guidance and the formulation of moral principles have been central to the development of human civilization. In recent centuries, particularly since the advent of the Enlightenment, there has been a marked shift towards humanistic approaches in ethics. These approaches prioritize human reason, autonomy, and individual rights as the primary sources of moral values and principles. While these developments have undoubtedly contributed to significant advancements in human rights, democracy, and the rule of law, they also reveal certain limitations when used as the sole foundation for ethical frameworks. This introduction explores these limitations and argues for the necessity of integrating transcendent principles to create a more comprehensive ethical framework.

Limitations of Humanistic Approaches to Ethics:

Subjectivity and Relativism:

Challenge: A strictly humanistic approach to ethics often leads to subjectivity and moral relativism. Without a transcendent reference point, ethical norms become contingent upon individual or cultural perspectives. This variability can fragment moral understanding and complicate the resolution of conflicting ethical claims.

Scope of Concern:

Challenge: Humanistic ethics, with its focus on individual rights and autonomy, sometimes fails to adequately address broader issues that extend beyond individual or immediate human concerns. This includes environmental ethics, animal rights, and the implications of technological advancements that impact the broader ecological and cosmic order.

Moral Motivation and Authority:

Challenge: In the absence of transcendent principles, the foundation for moral motivation and the authority of ethical imperatives can be significantly weakened. The reasoning behind moral actions may be reduced to social contract theories or utilitarian outcomes, which often fail to provide sufficient motivation for self-sacrifice or the pursuit of the common good, especially in the absence of direct personal benefit.

This chapter will delve deeper into these challenges, proposing a synthesis of transcendent principles drawn from both Abrahamic and Eastern traditions, aiming to enrich our modern ethical practices and governance models in the age of advanced technologies.

Transcendent Principles Discussed

1. Universalism and Objectivity: Transcendent principles, whether derived from divine command, the universal order, or natural law, offer a robust source of moral authority that transcends individual and cultural biases. These principles provide a universal framework that grounds ethical norms, furnishing a foundation for objective moral truths. By anchoring ethics in principles that surpass human subjectivity, we can establish guidelines that maintain consistency and integrity across various cultural and individual landscapes. This universality is crucial in a globalized world where cross-cultural interactions are commonplace and necessitates a common ethical language that can bridge diverse human experiences and values.

2. Integration with Ecological Systems: Transcendent ethics extend the scope of moral consideration beyond merely human interests to encompass a broader ecological perspective. By invoking principles that address more than human concerns, such ethics foster a deeper connection with the natural world. This holistic approach not only promotes environmental stewardship and interspecies respect but also encourages us to consider the long-term impacts of our actions on ecological systems. It invites us to view ourselves not as isolated agents but as integral components of a larger network of life, responsible for the well-being of the ecosystems that sustain us all.

3. Deepened Moral Motivation: Transcendent principles endow ethical actions with profound significance, anchoring moral duties in a commitment to higher orders or divine will. This alignment with something greater than oneself provides a powerful motivational force for ethical behavior, inspiring individuals to pursue virtuous actions not just for personal gain or immediate benefits but as part of a duty to the greater good. Such motivation is essential in fostering a sense of purpose and duty that transcends personal interests, encouraging actions that contribute positively to the community and the world at large.

Incorporating these transcendent principles into modern ethical discourse addresses the limitations of purely humanistic approaches and enriches our understanding and practice of ethics. This integration ensures that our actions are guided by values that honor both our heritage and our responsibilities to the future, reinforcing our commitment to ethical integrity in a complex, evolving world. As we explore these principles further in the context of governance and the ethical deployment of Generative AI, we find that they provide not only a counterbalance to the risks associated with advanced technologies but also a guiding light towards a more just and sustainable global society.

Abrahamic Thought: Divine Covenant and Moral Law

The Abrahamic traditions—Judaism, Christianity, and Islam—share a foundational belief in a transcendent God who not only creates the universe but also ordains a moral order for humanity. This section explores how each of these religions conceptualizes ethics through divine commandments, blending divine will with human reason, and examines the implications of submission to divine will as articulated by seminal thinkers within each tradition.

Judaism: Divine Commandments and Maimonides

In Judaism, the Torah is the cornerstone of ethical life, containing commandments (mitzvot) given by God to the Israelites. These commandments encompass a wide array of ethical, ritual, and societal laws, guiding not only religious observance but also daily moral conduct. Maimonides, a prominent figure in Jewish thought, stressed the rational aspects of the Torah's commandments. In his works "Mishneh Torah" and "Guide for the Perplexed," Maimonides argues that these divine commandments foster social harmony and personal integrity. He posits that adherence to these laws not only fulfills a covenant with God but also promotes ethical cultivation that aligns individuals with divine will, thus fostering a just and moral society.

Christianity: Divine Law and Aquinas

Christian ethics, deeply influenced by the teachings of Jesus Christ and the writings of the Apostles, focus on love, compassion, and redemption. Thomas Aquinas, a significant theologian in Christianity, sought to integrate Christian teachings with Aristotelian philosophy. In his "Summa Theologica," Aquinas introduces the concept of natural law, a moral understanding accessible to human reason and reflective of God's eternal law. For Aquinas, ethical living involves more than just adherence to divine commands; it requires active engagement of human reason to discern natural law. This synthesis of divine law and human reason provides a framework for Christians to live in harmony with God's will while navigating ethical dilemmas using rational faculties.

Islam: Submission to Divine Will and Al-Ghazali

Islam emphasizes submission (Islam) to the will of Allah, as revealed in the Qur'an and exemplified by the Prophet Muhammad. This submission encompasses all life aspects, including ethical conduct. Al-Ghazali, a notable theologian and mystic, significantly influenced Islamic ethics with his work "Ihya' 'Ulum al-Din" (The Revival of the Religious Sciences). He emphasizes the importance of purifying one's heart and intentions as a means to achieve closeness to God. For Al-Ghazali, ethical behavior arises from an internal state of submission to God's will, resulting in actions that reflect divine commandments and virtues. His approach underscores the relationship between external adherence to Islamic law (Sharia) and the internal cultivation of spiritual virtues (Tasawwuf), offering a comprehensive vision of Islamic ethics.

Eastern Thought: Cosmic Order and Paths to Enlightenment

Eastern philosophies offer diverse perspectives on ethics, each grounded in an understanding of a cosmic order and the individual's path to enlightenment. These traditions emphasize living in harmony with the universe, following natural laws, and cultivating virtues that lead to a balanced and ethical life. This section explores how Hinduism, Buddhism, Confucianism, and Taoism articulate these principles.

Hinduism: Dharma as Cosmic Law

In Hinduism, dharma represents the moral order that governs the universe and the individual's duty within it. It is an all-encompassing principle that dictates the correct way of living and ethical behavior, ensuring the stability and harmony of the world. Dharma varies according to one's age, caste, gender, and profession, yet it universally promotes virtues such as truthfulness, restraint, purity, and generosity. The Bhagavad Gita, a key text in Hinduism, emphasizes the importance of performing one's dharma without attachment to the outcomes, suggesting that ethical living is an offering to the divine and a path to liberation (moksha).

Buddhism: The Four Noble Truths and the Eightfold Path

Buddhism introduces a practical ethical system through the Four Noble Truths, which diagnose the human condition of suffering and its cessation through the Eightfold Path. This path provides guidelines for ethical living that align individuals with the natural order, encompassing right understanding, right intention, right speech, right action, right livelihood, right effort, right mindfulness, and right concentration. The emphasis on non-harm (ahimsa) and compassion extends beyond human interactions to include all living beings, reflecting a deep commitment to living in harmony with the natural world. The ethical life in Buddhism is not only about avoiding negative actions but actively cultivating positive qualities that lead to enlightenment and the liberation from suffering.

Confucianism: Harmony and Proper Conduct

Confucianism, with its focus on social harmony and the proper conduct of relationships, presents a vision of ethics rooted in the cosmic and social orders. The Five Cardinal Relationships (between ruler and subject, father and son, husband and wife, elder brother and younger brother, friend and friend) articulate the duties and virtues necessary for societal stability. Rituals (li) and benevolence (ren) are central to Confucian ethics, promoting a moral disposition towards others that is reflective of the harmony in the cosmos. For Confucius, ethical behavior arises not from adherence to a set of rules but from the cultivation of personal virtue and the maintenance of harmonious relationships.

Taoism: Alignment with the Tao

Taoism emphasizes living in accordance with the Tao, or the Way, which is the fundamental principle underlying and unifying the universe. The Tao is beyond definition but can be understood as the natural order of things. Taoist ethics, as articulated in the Tao Te Ching and the Zhuangzi, promote simplicity, spontaneity, and humility. The practice of wu-wei (non-action or effortless action) is central, suggesting that the most ethical way of living is one that is in harmony with the natural flow of the Tao. This approach values flexibility, pacifism, and environmental stewardship, advocating for a life that flows with, rather than against, the currents of the cosmos.

African Ethical Traditions: Ubuntu and Communal Harmony

African philosophies offer a rich tapestry of ethical insights, deeply rooted in the principles of communal relationships and collective well-being. Among these, Ubuntu stands out as a philosophy that emphasizes "I am because we are," underscoring the interconnectedness of individuals within their communities. Ubuntu promotes a way of life that respects the dignity, worth, and participation of every community member. In this view, ethical behavior supports the welfare of the community and is derived from the relationships that bind people together, rather than abstract codes or individualistic pursuits. This focus on communal harmony and moral responsibility is crucial in guiding ethical AI development, ensuring that technologies are used to enhance collective well-being and foster social cohesion.

Pacific Wisdom: Balance and Reciprocity

In many Pacific cultures, ethics are shaped by concepts of balance, reciprocity, and respect for both the natural world and social relationships. Traditional knowledge systems, often passed down through oral traditions and rituals, emphasize living in harmony with nature and maintaining social bonds through exchanges and mutual respect. For example, the Māori concept of *Tapu* (sacredness) and *Noa* (ordinary) governs interactions with people and the environment, promoting a respectful and balanced approach to both. These principles can inform ethical AI by advocating for systems that respect user privacy, promote data dignity, and balance technological advances with ecological and social integrity.

Pre-Columbian Ethical Frameworks: Cosmic Order and Community

The ethical systems of pre-Columbian civilizations such as the Aztecs, Mayans, and Incas were intricately linked to their cosmological views and communal lifestyles. For these societies, morality was often a reflection of cosmic order, with ethical norms derived from mythological narratives and observed natural cycles. Community well-being and the maintenance of harmony between the human, natural, and divine realms were paramount. These traditions emphasize the role of community in ethical deliberations and the importance of aligning human actions with broader cosmic principles. In the context of GenAI, this could translate into developing technologies that support communal decision-making and uphold principles of harmony and balance across various systems.

North American Indigenous Ethical Traditions: Relationship and Stewardship

North American Indigenous cultures present a diverse array of ethical frameworks, with a strong emphasis on the interconnectedness of life, the stewardship of the environment, and the maintenance of reciprocal relationships among people, and between people and nature. These ethical views are deeply rooted in a worldview that sees humans as integral parts of a larger ecological system, with responsibilities toward the land, water, plants, and animals—a concept often encapsulated in the belief in a web of life.

Sacred Responsibility and Earth Stewardship For many Indigenous tribes, such as the Navajo (Diné), Hopi, and Iroquois, life is a complex web of relationships that require respect and active maintenance. The notion of stewardship is not merely conservationist but is imbued with sacred duty. The land and all its constituents are considered relatives, not resources, which requires humans to engage in sustainable practices that promote the health of the land and all its beings. This understanding stresses the importance of long-term thinking and the consequences of actions that span generations.

The Principle of Reciprocity Reciprocity is another core component of Indigenous ethics, where the giving and receiving between individuals and nature are seen as fundamental to maintaining balance. This principle is not only about fair exchange but is a deeply ingrained practice of giving back to the community and the natural world, which supports the survival and well-being of all. In the context of GenAI, this principle would advocate for technologies that give back to the community, supporting societal and environmental health rather than merely extracting value.

Seven Generations Principle Many Indigenous cultures, including the Iroquois, operate under the "Seven Generations" stewardship, which teaches that decisions should be considered for their impact on the seventh generation into the future. This long-term perspective can inform ethical AI by guiding the development of technologies that ensure sustainability and benefit for future generations, promoting a deep, forward-thinking responsibility.

Introduction to AI-Generated Transcendent Ethics and Rules

In the quest to harmonize the vast diversity of cultural ethics into a cohesive framework, artificial intelligence (AI) can play a pivotal role by synthesizing universal principles from a broad array of human traditions. An AI model designed for this task would analyze and distill common ethical threads, creating a set of guidelines that reflect shared human values across different societies and historical contexts. These AI-generated rules aim to encapsulate fundamental principles that could guide human behavior towards a more harmonious and sustainable future.

Key Principles Identified by AI in Transcendent Ethics

Respect for Life and Interconnectedness: Across various cultures, a recurring emphasis is placed on the sanctity and interconnectedness of all life forms. This principle underlies many traditional ethical systems, advocating for a profound respect for nature and the myriad forms of life it sustains. An AI-generated ethical code would likely elevate this principle, proposing guidelines that prioritize the protection of life in all its diversity and the ecological systems upon which it depends. Such guidelines would advocate for environmental stewardship and emphasize our collective responsibility to ensure the health and well-being of our planet and its inhabitants.

The following pages contain examples of rules generated by AI.

Ethical Rule: "AI systems shall be designed and operated to preserve and enhance the ecological and biological systems of the Earth, respecting all forms of life and their interdependencies in decision-making processes."

Implementation of the Rule:

Design Considerations:

Impact Assessment: AI systems should include an ecological impact assessment tool that evaluates the potential environmental impacts of their deployment and operations. This tool would use data about biodiversity, ecosystem services, and environmental health to predict and mitigate negative impacts on ecosystems.

Biodiversity Algorithms: Develop algorithms that prioritize ecological health and biodiversity conservation. These could be used in resource management, urban planning, and agriculture to ensure that AI-supported activities contribute positively to the environment.

Operational Guidelines:

Sustainable Practices: AI operations must adhere to sustainability standards that minimize energy consumption, reduce waste, and utilize environmentally friendly materials and processes.

Ecological Data Integration: Integrate real-time environmental data to adjust operations in response to ecological feedback. For instance, AI in agriculture could adjust water usage based on local ecosystem needs to support nearby wetlands or wildlife.

Ethical Decision-Making Frameworks:

Stakeholder Engagement: Regularly consult with environmental scientists, local communities, and conservation groups to align AI operations with broader ecological health goals.

Ethical AI Review Boards: Establish multidisciplinary boards that include ecologists, ethicists, and community representatives to review and guide AI projects, ensuring they align with global ecological ethics and local environmental values.

Compliance and Monitoring:

Transparent Reporting: Implement transparent reporting mechanisms that publicly disclose the environmental impact of AI systems, including any breaches of ecological care standards.

Continuous Monitoring: Use sensors and remote monitoring to continuously assess the environmental impact of AI systems, allowing for real-time adjustments to mitigate unintended consequences.

Redress and Mitigation:

Impact Mitigation Fund: Create a fund supported by AI developers and users to finance environmental restoration projects where negative impacts from AI technologies are identified.

Feedback Mechanisms: Develop AI systems capable of adapting their operations based on feedback from ecological monitoring, ensuring dynamic responsiveness to environmental needs.

By adopting such a rule, GenAI can not only prevent harm to ecological and biological systems but actively contribute to their sustainability, demonstrating a global commitment to respecting life and interconnectedness. This approach aligns with the diverse ethical traditions, leveraging GenAI's capabilities to support an ethical framework that is not only globally inclusive but also actively beneficial to all forms of life on Earth.

Community and Social Harmony

From African Ubuntu to Confucian harmonious relationships and Indigenous practices of reciprocity, the importance of community welfare and social harmony is a recurring theme. A unified code might stress the importance of AI technologies that support community development, enhance social connections, and contribute to societal harmony rather than fostering division.

Ethical Rule: "AI systems shall be developed and deployed to enhance social cohesion and harmony, supporting community development and strengthening interpersonal relationships without promoting division or discord."

Implementation of the Rule:

Design Considerations:

Inclusivity in Design: Ensure AI systems are designed with input from diverse community groups, particularly underrepresented populations, to ensure their needs and perspectives are considered. This approach helps create technology that is universally beneficial and culturally sensitive.

Social Connection Algorithms: Develop algorithms that promote positive interactions and connections among users, enhancing understanding and cooperation across diverse social and cultural lines.

Operational Guidelines:

Community-Centric Deployment: AI technologies should be deployed in ways that support local community goals, such as improving public services, enhancing education, or boosting local economic activities without displacing local workers.

Harmony Metrics: Implement metrics to assess the impact of AI on social harmony, measuring variables such as community engagement, social cohesion, and public satisfaction.

Ethical Decision-Making Frameworks:

Multidisciplinary Teams: Include sociologists, community planners, and ethicists in the development teams to provide insights into the social dynamics and potential impacts of AI applications.

Ethical Review Processes: Establish review processes that specifically evaluate AI projects for their potential effects on social harmony and community welfare.

Compliance and Monitoring:

Impact Audits: Regularly conduct social impact audits to assess how AI deployments affect community welfare and social harmony, making adjustments based on findings.

Transparency and Reporting: Provide transparent reports to the public detailing how AI technologies are being used within communities and their effects on social relations.

Redress and Mitigation:

Community Feedback Loops: Create mechanisms for communities to provide ongoing feedback on AI technologies in use, including concerns about social disruption or harm.

Conflict Resolution Protocols: Develop protocols to address and resolve any conflicts or harms that arise from AI deployment, prioritizing restorative practices that mend social fabric and restore harmony.

By adhering to such a rule, GenAI can play a constructive role in fostering community development and enhancing social connections. This approach ensures that AI technologies contribute positively to societal harmony and are mindful of the complex social dynamics within communities. It aligns with global ethical traditions that value social cohesion and community well-being, ensuring that AI acts as a force for good in uniting and uplifting societies.

Justice and Fairness

Principles of justice and fairness appear universally, though conceptualized differently across cultures. An ethical code might incorporate these as fundamental principles, ensuring that AI systems are designed to promote equity, access, and fairness, and do not perpetuate or exacerbate existing inequalities.

Ethical Rule: "AI systems shall be developed and deployed to promote justice, fairness, and equity, ensuring that they contribute to the reduction of existing inequalities and do not create new forms of discrimination."

Implementation of the Rule:

Design Considerations:

Equitable Design: Develop AI systems that are accessible to all segments of society, including marginalized and underrepresented groups. This includes considering factors like affordability, accessibility, and cultural relevance in the design phase.

Bias Mitigation Algorithms: Integrate advanced algorithms specifically designed to detect and mitigate biases in AI decision-making processes, particularly in critical areas such as hiring, law enforcement, and loan approvals.

Operational Guidelines:

Diversity in Training Data: Ensure that the data used to train AI systems is diverse and representative of all demographics to prevent systemic biases. Regularly audit and update datasets to reflect changes in population demographics and social standards.

Fairness Audits: Conduct regular fairness audits of AI systems to assess their impact on different communities, identifying and correcting any disparities in treatment or outcomes.

Ethical Decision-Making Frameworks:

Inclusive Development Teams: Assemble development teams that are diverse in terms of gender, race, ethnicity, and socio-economic background to bring multiple perspectives to the design and implementation of AI systems.

Stakeholder Engagement: Engage with stakeholders, including those from affected communities, in the ethical review and decision-making processes to understand and integrate their concerns and insights.

Compliance and Monitoring:

Transparency Mechanisms: Implement mechanisms that ensure transparency in AI decision-making processes, allowing users to understand how decisions are made and on what basis.

Impact Reporting: Provide detailed reports on the societal impacts of AI, particularly concerning equity and fairness, to regulatory bodies and the public.

Redress and Mitigation:

Grievance Redressal Mechanisms: Establish robust mechanisms for individuals and communities to report perceived injustices or harms caused by AI systems, with clear pathways for redress and compensation.

Continuous Improvement: Ensure that feedback from fairness audits and grievance redressal feeds back into system design and operation, facilitating continuous improvement towards greater justice and fairness.

By committing to this ethical rule, GenAI technologies can be guided to not only avoid perpetuating existing inequalities but actively contribute to social justice and fairness. This approach ensures that AI systems are developed and used in a way that is fair, just, and equitable, reflecting the universal values of justice across diverse cultural contexts and contributing positively to societal well-being.

Transcendence and Higher Order Principles

Many traditions reference higher order or transcendental principles—be they divine laws, cosmic order, or universal dharma. Such principles could inform the development of AI ethics that transcend purely utilitarian or profit-driven motives, instead aligning with broader moral imperatives that guide long-term positive impacts.

Ethical Rule: "AI systems must be guided by transcendent principles that prioritize long-term societal well-being and moral imperatives beyond immediate profit or utility."

Implementation of the Rule:

Design Considerations:

Value-Aligned Design: Ensure that AI systems are designed with a core set of values that reflect transcendent principles, such as sustainability, human dignity, and social welfare. These values should guide all design choices, from data selection to algorithm development.

Long-Term Impact Analysis: Incorporate tools and methodologies that assess the long-term impacts of AI systems on society, the environment, and global ethics, ensuring that short-term gains do not undermine broader ethical objectives.

Operational Guidelines:

Sustainable Development Goals (SDGs) Integration: Align AI operations with global SDGs, ensuring that AI contributes positively to goals such as reducing inequality, promoting sustainable cities and communities, and ensuring responsible consumption and production.

Ethical Oversight: Establish oversight bodies composed of ethicists, community leaders, and other stakeholders who ensure that AI operations remain aligned with higher order principles.

Ethical Decision-Making Frameworks:

Transcendent Ethical Training: Provide training for AI developers and operators that focuses on ethical theories and principles that transcend cultural and immediate business concerns, fostering a deeper understanding of the ethical dimensions of AI.

Scenario Planning: Use scenario planning to explore the potential future impacts of AI technologies, considering both positive and negative outcomes to guide ethical decision-making.

Compliance and Monitoring:

Continuous Ethical Monitoring: Implement continuous monitoring systems that assess the ethical performance of AI systems against transcendent principles, adjusting operations as necessary to maintain alignment with these higher standards.

Transparency and Accountability: Maintain high levels of transparency in AI decision-making processes and outcomes, ensuring accountability to the public and stakeholders for ethical adherence.

Redress and Mitigation:

Ethical Audit Mechanisms: Regular ethical audits should be conducted to evaluate how well AI systems adhere to transcendent principles, with findings used to improve systems and address any deviations.

Community Engagement and Redress: Develop mechanisms for community feedback and engagement, ensuring that any harm or deviation from ethical standards can be quickly addressed and rectified.

By embedding these higher order principles into the core of GenAI development and operations, AI technologies can serve as instruments of ethical progress, fostering advancements that are not only technologically innovative but also deeply aligned with the broader moral imperatives that ensure long-term societal well-being. This rule supports the creation of AI systems that contribute positively to human and planetary flourishing, guided by a commitment to transcendent ethics that elevate their impact beyond mere functionality or profitability.

Integrity and Accountability

Integrity in action and clear accountability mechanisms are emphasized across various ethical frameworks. For AI, this could translate into the development of transparent systems where decision-making processes are clear, and mechanisms are in place for accountability and redress when harms occur.

Sustainability and Long-term Thinking

The Seven Generations principle of the Iroquois and similar long-term views in other cultures highlight the importance of considering the long-term consequences of actions. An ethical AI framework might include principles that require technologies to be assessed based on their long-term impacts on future generations and the sustainability of the planet.

Ethical Rule: "AI systems must be designed and implemented with a foresight that prioritizes sustainability and considers the long-term impacts on future generations and the planet."

Implementation of the Rule:

Design Considerations:

Sustainable Design: Develop AI systems with environmentally sustainable materials and practices, reducing the carbon footprint and resource usage across the lifecycle of AI technologies.

Future Impact Assessment: Incorporate assessments of long-term environmental, social, and economic impacts in the early design stages of AI systems to predict and mitigate potential negative consequences decades into the future.

Operational Guidelines:

Lifecycle Analysis: Conduct comprehensive lifecycle analyses of AI systems to ensure that all stages, from development to decommissioning, are aligned with sustainability goals.

Sustainable Operations: Implement operational practices that minimize energy consumption and waste in AI systems, utilizing green data centers, energy-efficient algorithms, and other sustainable technologies.

Ethical Decision-Making Frameworks:

Interdisciplinary Teams: Engage interdisciplinary teams that include environmental scientists, ethicists, and sustainability experts in the planning and development phases to ensure a holistic approach to sustainability.

Stakeholder Consultation: Consult with communities, especially indigenous and local populations, to understand the broader impacts of

AI on their environments and incorporate their insights into sustainability strategies.

Compliance and Monitoring:

Regular Sustainability Audits: Perform regular audits to ensure compliance with environmental standards and sustainability goals, adjusting practices as needed to improve sustainability outcomes.

Transparency in Sustainability Reporting: Provide transparent reporting on the environmental impact of AI operations, making data accessible to stakeholders and the public to foster accountability.

Redress and Mitigation:

Mitigation Plans: Develop and implement mitigation plans for any adverse long-term impacts identified during the lifecycle analysis or through stakeholder feedback.

Innovation in Sustainability: Encourage continuous innovation in sustainable technologies and practices within the AI field, leveraging advancements to reduce adverse impacts and enhance positive contributions to environmental stewardship.

By committing to this ethical rule, AI technologies can be developed and utilized in a manner that not only respects current environmental and social norms but also proactively considers the well-being of future generations. This long-term, sustainable approach ensures that AI acts as a force for positive change, supporting the ongoing health of the planet and promoting a legacy of responsibility and care for the natural world. Such a commitment aligns with the Seven Generations principle and similar cultural values that emphasize the importance of foresight and long-term accountability in technological development.

Adaptability and Cultural Sensitivity

Recognizing the diversity of cultural values and norms, an effective ethical AI framework would need to be adaptable to different cultural contexts. This would involve incorporating flexibility in ethical guidelines to respect and reflect diverse cultural practices and priorities.

Ethical Rule: "AI systems must be designed and operated with an inherent adaptability that respects and reflects the diversity of cultural values and norms, ensuring that ethical guidelines are flexible and contextually relevant."

Implementation of the Rule:

Design Considerations:

Culturally Inclusive Design: Develop AI systems that are sensitive to cultural differences by involving cultural experts in the design process. This includes accommodating various languages, social norms, and cultural practices.

Customizable Ethical Parameters: Allow for the customization of AI behavior and ethics settings to align with local cultural norms and values, ensuring that AI systems can operate effectively and respectfully in diverse settings.

Operational Guidelines:

Cultural Adaptation Protocols: Implement protocols that enable AI systems to adapt their operations based on the cultural context in which they are deployed. This may involve dynamic adjustments to interaction styles, decision-making processes, and content presentation.

Continuous Cultural Learning: Equip AI systems with mechanisms to learn from their interactions in different cultural environments, continuously improving their cultural sensitivity and effectiveness.

Ethical Decision-Making Frameworks:

Cultural Impact Assessments: Regularly conduct cultural impact assessments to understand how AI technologies affect different cultural groups and to identify potential areas of cultural friction.

Diverse Stakeholder Engagement: Engage a broad spectrum of stakeholders from diverse cultural backgrounds in the development and review of AI systems to ensure that multiple perspectives are considered.

Compliance and Monitoring:

Monitoring Cultural Impact: Continuously monitor the cultural impact of AI systems, assessing whether they remain sensitive to and respectful of cultural diversity.

Independent Cultural Audits: Utilize independent audits to evaluate the cultural sensitivity of AI systems, providing an external perspective on their effectiveness and areas for improvement.

Redress and Mitigation:

Responsive Adaptation Mechanisms: Develop mechanisms to respond swiftly to cultural insensitivity identified either through user feedback or monitoring systems. This includes the ability to update or modify AI systems to better align with cultural expectations.

Community-Based Feedback Loops: Establish feedback loops with communities to gather ongoing input on AI system performance and impact, ensuring that AI technologies adapt to evolving cultural norms and values.

By embedding adaptability and cultural sensitivity into the core of AI development and operations, AI technologies can be more effectively integrated into various cultural contexts, enhancing their acceptance and effectiveness. This approach not only respects the diversity of global cultures but also enriches AI systems with a broader range of human experiences and perspectives, enhancing their utility and ethical alignment. This rule supports the creation of AI that is not only globally operational but also locally respected and valued, fostering a deeper integration of technology into diverse human environments.

Moral Education and Development

Many traditions not only set out what is right or wrong but also emphasize the cultivation of virtue and moral character. In the context of AI, this could suggest a focus on developing systems that support ethical education and promote the development of moral reasoning in users, not just compliance with predefined rules.

Ethical Rule: "AI systems must be designed to support and enhance ethical education and the development of moral reasoning in users, going beyond mere rule compliance to foster a deeper understanding and cultivation of ethical principles."

Implementation of the Rule:

Design Considerations:

Educational AI Features: Integrate educational features into AI systems that teach users about ethical principles and moral reasoning through interactive scenarios, quizzes, and decision-making simulations.

Virtue-Enhancing Algorithms: Develop algorithms that are programmed to encourage and reinforce virtuous behaviors and decisions, based on ethical theories and frameworks from diverse cultural perspectives.

Operational Guidelines:

User-Centric Learning Modules: Create user-centric, customizable learning modules within AI applications that adapt to the individual's learning pace and style, focusing on ethical dilemmas and virtue cultivation.

Contextual Ethics Prompts: Implement contextual prompts within AI systems that encourage users to consider ethical dimensions and consequences of their actions in real-time, enhancing moral awareness.

Ethical Decision-Making Frameworks:

Ethics Advisory Panels: Establish ethics advisory panels composed of ethicists, cultural scholars, and psychologists to guide the development of AI's moral education functionalities.

Continuous Ethics Training: Incorporate continuous ethics training programs for AI developers and managers to ensure they are equipped to integrate ethical considerations effectively into AI design and deployment.

Compliance and Monitoring:

Ethical Usage Tracking: Monitor how users interact with ethical education features in AI systems to assess their effectiveness and make necessary adjustments.

Impact Assessments: Regularly perform impact assessments to evaluate how effectively AI systems are enhancing ethical understanding and moral reasoning among users.

Redress and Mitigation:

Feedback Mechanisms: Develop and maintain robust feedback mechanisms that allow users to report concerns or suggestions related to the ethical functionalities of AI systems.

Iterative Improvements: Use feedback and assessment outcomes to make iterative improvements to AI systems, ensuring they remain effective as tools for moral education and development.

By prioritizing moral education and the development of ethical reasoning, AI technologies can contribute positively to societal moral standards, fostering a more ethically aware population. This approach aligns with the educational mandates of various ethical traditions that emphasize the cultivation of virtue and character. AI systems designed with these principles can support a broader societal commitment to ethical behavior, enriching the moral fabric of communities and enhancing the overall effectiveness of ethical guidelines in technology use. This commitment to moral education within AI development not only improves individual user engagement with ethical issues but also bolsters the societal capacity to address complex moral challenges in an increasingly AI-integrated world.

Conclusion

This chapter has explored the profound and varied ethical insights from global philosophical and religious traditions, providing a rich tapestry of moral principles that can inform and guide the governance of GenAI.

From the transcendent mandates of Abrahamic faiths to the holistic ethics of Eastern philosophies, and the community-focused values of African, Pacific, pre-Columbian, and North American Indigenous cultures, each tradition offers unique perspectives that enhance our understanding of ethical AI.

Transcendent Principles and Universalism highlighted the importance of transcending narrow, culturally-bound ethical considerations to embrace universal principles that address broader human concerns. These principles are crucial for developing AI systems that are not only technologically advanced but also morally attuned to the complexities of global and ecological ethics.

Integrity and Accountability stressed the need for AI systems to operate with transparency and for developers to be accountable for the impacts of their technologies. This ensures that AI not only adheres to ethical norms but is also responsive to the societal consequences of its deployment.

Adaptability and Cultural Sensitivity emphasized the significance of designing AI systems that respect and adapt to the diverse cultural landscapes in which they operate. This adaptability ensures that AI technologies are inclusive and respectful of cultural differences, enhancing their global applicability and acceptance.

Sustainability and Long-term Thinking urged the integration of sustainability into AI development processes, reflecting the ethical commitment to future generations and the health of our planet. This long-term perspective is essential for ensuring that AI technologies contribute positively to our world without causing irreversible damage.

Moral Education and Development discussed the potential of AI to foster moral and ethical development among users, moving beyond compliance to cultivate a deeper understanding and appreciation of ethical behavior. This is aligned with the global ethical imperative to not only live by rules but to understand and internalize them.

As we advance into the era of AI, it is imperative that we draw on these rich ethical traditions to formulate a governance model that is as culturally informed and ethically robust as it is technologically sophisticated. The convergence of these diverse ethical viewpoints provides a more holistic and nuanced framework that can guide the development and application of AI in a way that respects human dignity, promotes societal welfare, and navigates the complex moral landscape of our time.

Part V : Quantum Computing

Chapter 15: The Infinite Frontier: Quantum Computing and GenAI

The intersection of GenAI and quantum computing represents a transformative leap in computational capabilities, pushing the frontiers of what machines can learn, solve, and create. This chapter outlines the synergistic relationship between these two revolutionary technologies, exploring their combined potential to accelerate innovation and address complex challenges that are currently beyond reach. It also speculates on future applications and considers the theoretical limits and societal implications of this convergence.

A Brief Explanation of Quantum Computing

Quantum computing represents a significant shift in how data is processed, leveraging the principles of quantum mechanics to enhance computational speeds and capabilities far beyond what is possible with classical computing. Central to this technology is the concept of superposition, a fundamental principle of quantum mechanics that enables quantum bits, or qubits, to operate in ways traditional bits cannot.

Understanding Superposition in Quantum Computing

Superposition allows a qubit to exist in multiple states simultaneously. Whereas a classical bit can be either 0 or 1, a qubit can be in a state that is 0, 1, or any quantum superposition of these states. This means a qubit can represent and process a large number of possibilities at once. When multiple qubits act in concert, this ability is exponentially increased. For example, while two classical bits can represent any one of four possible combinations (00, 01, 10, 11) at any one time, two qubits can represent all four combinations simultaneously due to superposition.

This characteristic drastically enhances the data processing capability of quantum computers:

Parallelism: Superposition enables quantum computers to perform many calculations at once. Where a classical computer would compute each possibility sequentially, a quantum computer can process all possibilities simultaneously. This parallelism allows quantum computers to solve certain types of problems much more quickly than classical computers.

Complex Simulations: Quantum computers can simulate complex systems more efficiently than classical computers. In fields such as quantum chemistry or material science, where behavior at the quantum level significantly impacts the system, classical computers struggle to simulate such systems accurately because of the computational load. Quantum computers, thanks to superposition, can handle the exponential growth of variables without a corresponding increase in processing time.

Enhanced Optimization: Superposition allows quantum algorithms to explore a vast search space more comprehensively than classical algorithms. For problems where there are many possible configurations (such as optimization problems, scheduling, and routing), quantum computers can assess multiple possibilities at once, finding solutions faster and more efficiently than their classical counterparts.

Implications for GenAI

For GenAI, the ability of quantum computing to leverage superposition means that AI models can be trained on larger datasets, analyze more variables simultaneously, and possibly develop more nuanced understandings and outputs than ever before. The integration of quantum computing could lead to breakthroughs in how AI understands complex systems, including human language, environmental systems, and biological processes.

Quantum-enhanced GenAI could potentially model real-world phenomena at a level of detail that is impossible with current AI, leading to more accurate predictions and more effective solutions in areas like climate modeling, economic forecasting, and personalized medicine.

Quantum Computing and GenAI: Redefining Foundations of Discovery

In the realm of human cognition, our understanding of complex systems is often constrained by an innate predisposition towards linear cause-and-effect reasoning. Similarly, traditional computing has been limited by its foundational binary structure, where operations are performed on discrete bits that represent either a zero or a one. However, the convergence of quantum computing and GenAI promises to transcend these limitations, ushering in a new paradigm of knowledge exploration and discovery.

Beyond Binary: The Quantum Leap

Quantum computing introduces a radical shift from traditional binary systems. Utilizing qubits, which can exist in multiple states simultaneously thanks to quantum superposition, quantum computers are not confined to binary on-off states. This capability allows them to perform complex calculations and analyze vast datasets far more efficiently than classical computers.

Generative AI and Multidimensional Analysis

GenAI complements quantum computing by its ability to learn from data and generate new, previously unseen patterns and ideas. Unlike humans, who typically process information sequentially and within the confines of known relationships, GenAI can assess multiple data streams simultaneously and identify connections across disparate domains. This capability is further enhanced by quantum computing, which can feed GenAI with a higher volume and variety of data at unprecedented speeds.

Creating Foundations for Cross-Domain Discoveries

The synergy between quantum computing and GenAI could create a new foundation for discovery, characterized by 'combinations of combinations'—a multi-layered, cross-disciplinary approach that mirrors the interconnected complexity of the natural world. This new model of discovery is predicated on the idea that innovation often occurs at the intersection of fields, where seemingly unrelated concepts and datasets intersect leading to breakthroughs in numerous complex and global challenges:

Climate Change and Environmental Management: Quantum-enhanced GenAI could revolutionize our approach to environmental management and climate change mitigation. By analyzing vast datasets encompassing weather patterns, pollution levels, and ecological dynamics simultaneously, these systems could predict environmental changes with unprecedented accuracy and suggest more effective interventions. For instance, they might optimize renewable energy deployment across the globe or model the impact of specific conservation strategies on biodiversity.

Healthcare and Medicine: In healthcare, the combination of quantum computing and GenAI could lead to personalized medicine on a scale never before feasible. This could include the ability to analyze genetic data alongside environmental factors and lifestyle choices to tailor medical treatments to individual patients. Additionally, quantum computing could enable the simulation of complex biological processes that would help in discovering new drugs and treatment protocols much faster than current capabilities.

Material Science: By enabling the simulation of materials at the quantum level, this synergy could lead to the creation of new materials with customized properties. For example, ultra-strong lightweight materials for better fuel efficiency in vehicles, or new semiconductors that could pave the way for more efficient electronic devices.

Energy Storage and Conversion: Addressing the global need for clean energy, quantum-enhanced GenAI could develop new battery technologies and energy conversion systems. These systems could efficiently store renewable energy or convert carbon dioxide into useful products, significantly impacting efforts to reduce greenhouse gas emissions.

Financial Modeling: Quantum computing could transform financial modeling and risk management, allowing for the real-time simulation of complex economic scenarios. GenAI could enhance these models with predictive analytics, offering insights into market trends and economic impacts with a degree of precision and speed unattainable today.

Space Exploration and Astrophysics: The capabilities of GenAI combined with quantum computing could vastly enhance our ability to model and understand the universe. This might lead to new insights into dark matter, black holes, or even the potential for life on other planets, as well as optimizing space missions and satellite deployments.

Urban Planning and Smart Cities: In urban planning, quantum-enhanced GenAI could lead to the creation of "smart cities," where infrastructure systems are optimized for energy use, traffic flow, public safety, and sustainability. This technology could plan cities that dynamically adapt to changes in population and resource use, minimizing environmental impacts and improving quality of life.

Social Systems: Finally, by modeling complex social interactions and the potential outcomes of different social policies, this technological synergy could help mankind understand the potential impacts of their decisions on social equity, education, and public health.

These areas are just the beginning of what might be possible when the boundaries between disciplines blur, facilitated by the advanced capabilities of quantum computing and GenAI. The potential for cross-domain solutions could lead to a new era of discovery and problem-solving, echoing the broad and impactful innovations of the greatest polymaths of history.

Supercharged Data Analysis: Quantum computers can analyze large datasets much faster than classical computers, enabling GenAI to learn from larger datasets more quickly. This could lead to more sophisticated and accurate AI models that can, for example, better predict weather patterns or optimize complex systems like large-scale logistics.

Complex Problem Solving: Quantum computing can perform complex calculations at unprecedented speeds, potentially solving problems considered intractable for classical computers. This capability could be harnessed by GenAI to explore solutions in fields such as cryptography, materials science, and pharmaceuticals, where traditional algorithms fall short.

Enhanced Creativity and Innovation: By processing information in fundamentally novel ways, quantum computing could enable GenAI systems to generate more innovative and creative solutions across various domains like art, music, and design, transcending the current creativity limitations of AI.

A New Era of Cognitive Exploration

The integration of quantum computing and GenAI represents not just a technological upgrade but a conceptual revolution. It mirrors the leap from the Earth-centric to a heliocentric view of our solar system, redefining what is possible within the domains of science, technology, and human understanding. Just as the polymaths of the past crossed the boundaries of disciplines using the tools and theories available to them, this new technological synergy will navigate across a broader expanse of knowledge, uncovering new realms of discovery and providing solutions to some of the most pressing challenges facing humanity today. By doing so, it not only expands our capacity for knowledge but fundamentally reshapes the foundations upon which we build future innovations and understand the universe.

Chapter 16: A New Era or the Final Chapter?

The convergence of quantum computing and GenAI may not only signify the dawn of a new era of technological advancement but also prompt us to consider whether this could be the ultimate phase of human technological evolution. As these technologies push the boundaries of what can be computed or engineered, they compel us to reassess our roles and responsibilities in a world where our creations might surpass human capacities in specific areas. This chapter explores these profound implications and emphasizes the importance of navigating this new frontier with foresight and responsibility.

Quantum Artificial Life: Bridging GenAI and Quantum Computing

The integration of quantum computing with GenAI opens new frontiers in the simulation of complex life-like behaviors and evolutionary processes. Leveraging the unique properties of quantum mechanics, such as superposition and entanglement, GenAI can achieve simulations of biological systems with unparalleled precision and complexity, far surpassing the capabilities of classical computing systems.

Enhancing Life Simulations with Quantum Capabilities

Quantum computers use qubits that can represent multiple states simultaneously, enabling them to perform numerous calculations at once. This immense processing power can dramatically enhance the capabilities of GenAI in several ways:

Complex System Modeling: Quantum-enhanced GenAI can model intricate biological systems at a molecular or even quantum level, capturing detailed interactions within ecosystems or genetic networks. These models can accurately predict the ripple effects of minor changes across an entire system, which is crucial for advancing our understanding in fields such as genetics, ecology, and evolutionary biology.

Evolutionary Algorithms: Utilizing quantum computing, GenAI can simulate evolutionary processes by exploring countless genetic variations and environmental scenarios simultaneously. This could lead to deeper insights into how specific traits or behaviors evolved under various pressures and predict potential future evolutionary paths.

Artificial Life Forms: In a quantum computing framework, GenAI can create and evolve virtual organisms within complex and dynamically changing environments. These simulations allow artificial life forms to adapt and evolve, offering a window into the fundamental principles of life and the adaptability of biological entities under different environmental conditions.

Ethical and Philosophical Implications

The development of quantum artificial life is not just a technological advance but also a venture into profound ethical and philosophical territory:

Responsibility and Control: As these systems become more complex and autonomous, it becomes increasingly important to establish clear guidelines on who is responsible for their outcomes. This includes ensuring that quantum artificial life technologies are developed and used within ethical boundaries to prevent misuse.

The Nature of Life: The capability to simulate life processes with such high fidelity may challenge our existing definitions and understandings of life. If artificial systems begin to exhibit characteristics typically associated with natural organisms, such as adaptation or self-organization, it could lead to significant philosophical debates about the essence of life and the rights of artificial entities.

The exploration of quantum artificial life through GenAI not only pushes the boundaries of scientific and technological capabilities but also encourages us to reconsider some of the fundamental philosophical questions about life and existence. As we venture further into this domain, the convergence of quantum computing and GenAI promises to redefine our approach to understanding complex biological and ecological systems, while also posing significant ethical challenges that must be navigated with care and consideration.

The development and application of quantum artificial life through GenAI touch upon several fundamental philosophical questions about life and existence, challenging our existing frameworks and prompting a reevaluation of deeply held beliefs. These questions span the nature of life, the criteria for consciousness, and the ethical treatment of artificial entities.

Then, What is Life?

Traditionally, life has been characterized by criteria such as growth, reproduction, and response to stimuli. However, quantum artificial life, which may exhibit some but not all traditional life characteristics, challenges these definitions. For instance, if a quantum-computed model can evolve, adapt, and self-organize, does it qualify as "alive"? This question invites us to consider whether life is defined by its biochemical basis or the presence of certain life-like behaviors, regardless of the underlying medium.

Consciousness and Sentience

The possibility that quantum-enhanced GenAI systems could one day exhibit behaviors akin to learning, memory, or even decision-making leads to questions about consciousness and sentience:

Consciousness: Could these systems ever become conscious? If quantum mechanics allows for complex interactions at a scale and speed unachievable by classical systems, might this enable a form of consciousness distinct from biological awareness?

Sentience: If a system demonstrates predictive or adaptive behaviors that suggest a form of "understanding," does this imply sentience? How we answer this influences how we ethically consider these systems, particularly in terms of rights or protections they might warrant.

Ethical Considerations of Creating and Interacting with Artificial Life

The development of artificial life raises significant ethical considerations:

Rights of Artificial Entities: If an artificial system reaches a complexity that seems to mimic life, what moral obligations do we have towards it? This includes considerations of harm, rights to existence or termination, and the potential for suffering.

Dual Use and Control: As with all powerful technologies, there is potential for both beneficial and detrimental uses. The capability to simulate and potentially manipulate life processes can have profound implications for medicine, ecology, and biology, but also poses risks such as bioethical breaches or unintended ecological impacts.

Responsibility Towards Our Creations

Quantum artificial life systems, particularly those that might learn or evolve, require us to consider our responsibilities as creators:

Creator Responsibility: What responsibilities do we have for the actions or outcomes of our creations? This encompasses not only the direct impacts of these systems but also their long-term effects on societal, ecological, and global scales.

Sustainability and Legacy: The long-term implications of introducing sophisticated artificial systems into the environment, their demands on resources, and their integration with natural systems must be considered to ensure sustainable and beneficial outcomes.

Rethinking Our Place in the Universe

Finally, the advent of quantum artificial life forces us to rethink humanity's place within the universe. If we are not unique in our ability to exhibit complex, life-like behaviors or develop cognitive processes, what does this mean for our understanding of human exceptionalism? This reevaluation can influence everything from our philosophical outlook to practical policies regarding technology, environment, and extraterrestrial life.

These philosophical explorations are essential as they not only guide the development and deployment of technologies like quantum artificial life but also shape our broader understanding of life, consciousness, and our ethical responsibilities in an increasingly complex world.

Theoretical Limits

Quantum computing is still in its infancy, grappling with several challenges that define its theoretical and practical limits. As we explore the integration of quantum capabilities with GenAI, it is crucial to understand these boundaries to fully harness their potential.

Quantum Decoherence and Error Rates

One of the most significant hurdles in quantum computing is the high error rates due to quantum decoherence. Quantum bits, or qubits, must maintain their quantum state to perform computations effectively. However, qubits are highly sensitive to their environment, which can lead to decoherence, where qubits lose their quantum properties. This phenomenon significantly impacts the reliability and scalability of quantum computations, posing a fundamental limit to the complexity and duration of computations that can be effectively managed.

Qubit Coherence Time

Coherence time refers to the duration over which qubits can maintain their quantum state. Prolonging coherence time is fundamental to performing longer and more complex quantum operations necessary for advanced GenAI applications. Extending coherence times beyond current capabilities is a theoretical and practical challenge that quantum physicists and engineers are actively trying to solve, using advanced materials and innovative qubit design and isolation techniques.

Scalability Challenges

Scaling quantum systems by adding more qubits presents another theoretical limit. The power of quantum computing increases exponentially with the addition of each qubit; however, maintaining the stability and coherence of a large-scale quantum system is a complex engineering challenge. Achieving this scalability is essential for quantum computing to realize its potential across broader applications, including GenAI.

Quantum Algorithm Limits

The development of quantum algorithms that can exploit quantum mechanical properties such as superposition and entanglement is still in progress. Current quantum algorithms, such as Shor's algorithm for factorization and Grover's algorithm for database searching, showcase the potential of quantum computing. However, creating algorithms that can fully utilize these properties for GenAI tasks remains a significant theoretical and practical challenge.

Fundamental Quantum Mechanics

Quantum mechanics itself imposes limits on what quantum computing can achieve. Principles like the no-cloning theorem, which states that it is impossible to create an identical copy of an arbitrary unknown quantum state, and the uncertainty principle, which limits the precision with which certain pairs of physical properties, like position and momentum, can be simultaneously known, inherently bound the capabilities of quantum computing.

Understanding these theoretical limits is crucial as we continue to explore the integration of quantum computing with GenAI. These limits not only define the scope of potential applications but also guide the development of technologies that are both feasible and practically implementable within the framework of quantum mechanics.

Ethical Implications

The integration of quantum computing with GenAI not only offers transformative potential but also presents significant ethical challenges that need careful consideration and proactive governance. Drawing from concepts explored in Chapter 16 on using traditional cultural foundations to mitigate human bias, we can explore how quantum-enhanced GenAI might be governed by an ethical framework that incorporates these age-old wisdoms alongside modern ethical considerations.

Privacy and Data Security

With quantum computing's potential to process data at unprecedented speeds, privacy concerns escalate, particularly around the ability to decrypt previously secure communications. Here, principles from traditional ethics about the sanctity of personal space and confidentiality can guide the development of new encryption technologies that respect individual privacy, aligning with both technological capability and ethical imperatives.

Surveillance and Bias

The enhanced capability for surveillance with quantum-enhanced GenAI systems raises concerns about the misuse of data and increased monitoring capabilities. Ethical frameworks based on principles of justice and fairness, as seen in various cultural traditions, can inform guidelines that prevent the misuse of surveillance technologies and ensure they are used to promote societal welfare rather than control. Additionally, incorporating diverse cultural perspectives can help identify and mitigate biases in AI algorithms, ensuring that these systems serve all segments of society equitably.

Employment and Societal Impact

The potential job displacement due to automation by quantum-enhanced GenAI systems needs ethical frameworks that consider the long-term welfare of affected individuals. Drawing on principles like the community and social harmony found in both Abrahamic and Eastern traditions, policies could be designed to support transitions for workers impacted by automation, emphasizing the creation of opportunities that align with human dignity and societal well-being.

Dual Use and Weaponization

The risk of dual-use applications of quantum-enhanced GenAI, where technology can be used for both beneficial and harmful purposes, requires robust ethical governance. This governance can be informed by transcendent principles that prioritize life and integrity, guiding the development and deployment of these technologies in a manner that prevents their misuse. International cooperation, inspired by principles of global harmony and peace found in various cultural traditions, will be crucial in regulating and overseeing the use of such powerful technologies.

Long-term Societal Changes

The profound societal impacts anticipated from the deployment of quantum-enhanced GenAI necessitate a governance approach that is flexible and adaptable, incorporating long-term thinking and sustainability—a principle echoed in many traditional cultures, such as the Iroquois' Seventh Generation principle. Policies should be crafted to ensure that technological advancements contribute positively to the social fabric, enhancing human life and the ecological balance.

Ethical AI Governance Using GenAI

Integrating GenAI into the governance process itself could help in applying these ethical principles more effectively. GenAI systems, enhanced by quantum computing, can be designed to monitor and audit AI applications continuously, ensuring adherence to ethical standards and mitigating human biases in real-time. Such systems could act as guardians of ethical AI use, programmed to align with both modern and traditional ethical standards to ensure they reflect a balanced perspective that respects human rights, cultural diversity, and global ethical norms.

Incorporating these traditional principles into the governance of quantum-enhanced GenAI not only helps address the ethical implications but also aligns technological advancements with human values, ensuring that these powerful tools are used to foster a just, equitable, and harmonious society.

The Responsibility of Harnessing GenAI

The immense capabilities of GenAI entail significant responsibilities. As we navigate this ethical landscape—from privacy concerns to addressing the digital divide and potential job displacement—the governance of GenAI demands global cooperation, transparency, and the creation of comprehensive frameworks that prioritize human welfare.

Harnessing GenAI responsibly also involves recognizing its limitations and the irreplaceable value of human insight, empathy, and moral judgment. It calls for a synergistic relationship between human and artificial intelligence, where each complements the other to achieve outcomes that are not only technologically advanced but also socially responsible and aligned with ethical norms.

A Collaborative Path Forward

The journey toward a future shaped by GenAI and quantum computing is inherently collaborative, necessitating the active participation of technologists, ethicists, policymakers, and the global community. This endeavor requires a commitment to education and lifelong learning, ensuring that all individuals have the tools to thrive in a transformed world. Moreover, it demands a focus on inclusivity, ensuring that the benefits of these technologies are accessible to everyone, thereby bridging gaps rather than exacerbating them.

Envisioning the Future

As we stand on the brink of this new technological era, our approach should be one of cautious optimism. We envision a future where GenAI acts as a catalyst for positive change—driving innovation while adhering to ethical standards and promoting a just and equitable society. The path we choose now will set the foundation for how these technologies reshape our world and reflect our values and aspirations.

Conclusion for this Book

This exploration of the GenAI revolution has taken us through the transformative impacts of AI across various domains—from enhancing workflows and creative processes in the early chapters to redefining ethical standards and governance models in later discussions. As we delved into the integration of GenAI with quantum computing, we uncovered both the extraordinary potential of these technologies and the significant ethical and social challenges they present.

As we conclude, we find ourselves at a pivotal moment in history. The integration of quantum computing and GenAI presents a horizon rich with potential yet fraught with challenges. How we choose to navigate this landscape will determine the legacy of our era—whether these technologies will ultimately serve to amplify our human experience or lead us into uncharted territories of ethical and social dilemmas. The future is not predetermined; it is ours to shape.

The immense capabilities of GenAI entail significant responsibilities. As we navigate this ethical landscape—from privacy concerns to addressing the digital divide and potential job displacement—the governance of GenAI demands global cooperation, transparency, and the creation of comprehensive frameworks that prioritize human welfare.

Harnessing GenAI responsibly also involves recognizing its limitations and the irreplaceable value of human insight, empathy, and moral judgment. It calls for a synergistic relationship between human and artificial intelligence, where each complements the other to achieve outcomes that are not only technologically advanced but also socially responsible and aligned with ethical norms.

The journey toward a future shaped by GenAI and quantum computing is inherently collaborative, necessitating the active participation of technologists, ethicists, policymakers, and the global community. This endeavor requires a commitment to education and lifelong learning, ensuring that all individuals have the tools to thrive in a transformed world. Moreover, it demands a focus on inclusivity, ensuring that the benefits of these technologies are accessible to everyone, thereby bridging gaps rather than exacerbating them.

We envision a future where GenAI acts as a catalyst for positive change—driving innovation while adhering to ethical standards and promoting a just and equitable society. Let us steer towards a future where technology enhances our humanity and fosters global well-being, reflecting our deepest values and highest aspirations in the quantum age. This is our challenge and our opportunity as we stand on the threshold of what could be the greatest era of discovery or the final chapter in our technological evolution.

Appendices

Appendix A: Glossary of Terms Used in the Book

Abrahamic Traditions: Religions, including Judaism, Christianity, and Islam, which trace their origins to the patriarch Abraham.

Autonomy: The right or condition of self-government, especially in a particular sphere.

Cultural Sensitivity: Awareness of and sensitivity to the differences and diversity within and between cultures.

Digital Divide: The gap between those who have ready access to computers and the internet, and those who do not.

Eastern Philosophies: Philosophical thoughts originating from East and Southeast Asia, including Confucianism, Taoism, Buddhism, and Hinduism.

Ethical AI: The branch of ethics concerned with the moral implications and responsibilities involved in the development and application of artificial intelligence technologies.

GenAI: Artificial intelligence technologies that can generate new content, ideas, or data based on their training data and algorithms.

Governance: The processes, rules, and practices through which decisions are made, authority is exercised, and accountability is ensured.

Holistic: Emphasizing the importance of the whole and the interdependence of its parts, rather than the parts separately.

Integrity: The quality of being honest and having strong moral principles; moral uprightness.

Interconnectedness: The state of being connected with each other, emphasizing the relationships and dependencies among various elements in a system.

Job Displacement: The loss of jobs caused by technological innovation, especially when tasks performed by humans are replaced by machines or software.

Quantum Artificial Life: A theoretical concept in which quantum computing is used to simulate complex life-like behaviors and evolutionary processes.

Quantum Coherence: The quality of a quantum state being in a superposition of multiple states simultaneously in a system free of any external interference.

Quantum Computing: A type of computing that uses quantum-mechanical phenomena, such as superposition and entanglement, to perform operations on data.

Quantum Enhanced GenAI: GenAI systems that leverage quantum computing to improve their capabilities beyond traditional computational limits.

Quantum Entanglement: A physical phenomenon that occurs when pairs or groups of particles are generated, interact, or share spatial proximity in ways such that the quantum state of each particle cannot be described independently of the state of the others, even when the particles are separated by a large distance.

Quantum Mechanics: A fundamental theory in physics that provides a description of the physical properties of nature at the scale of atoms and subatomic particles.

Qubit: The basic unit of quantum information—the quantum version of the classical binary bit, which can represent and store information in both 0 and 1 simultaneously, thanks to superposition.

Sustainability: The ability to be maintained at a certain rate or level; avoidance of the depletion of natural resources to maintain ecological balance.

Superposition: A fundamental principle of quantum mechanics that allows particles to be in a combination of all possible states at once, as opposed to a definite state.

Theoretical Limits: The conceptual boundaries that define the maximum possible capabilities of a technology based on current scientific understanding.

Transcendent: Going beyond ordinary limits; surpassing; exceeding.

Appendix B: Resources for Further Exploration

"Superintelligence: Paths, Dangers, Strategies" by Nick Bostrom

Explores the risks and potential of artificial intelligence, particularly focusing on the scenarios where AI surpasses human intelligence.

"The Master Algorithm: How the Quest for the Ultimate Learning Machine Will Remake Our World" by Pedro Domingos

Offers insights into machine learning and the potential of a 'master algorithm' that could explain everything given enough data.

"AI Superpowers: China, Silicon Valley, and the New World Order" by Kai-Fu Lee

Discusses the rise of AI, focusing on how it's shaping the economic and geopolitical landscapes between the U.S. and China.

"Architects of Intelligence: The Truth About AI from the People Building It" by Martin Ford

Contains detailed interviews with major players in the AI field, discussing the future prospects and ethical challenges of AI.

"Weapons of Math Destruction: How Big Data Increases Inequality and Threatens Democracy" by Cathy O'Neil

Explores how big data and algorithms, if not carefully managed, could increase inequality and threaten democratic systems.

"Hello World: Being Human in the Age of Algorithms" by Hannah Fry

Examines how algorithms and AI are involved in our everyday lives and discusses their impact on our future.

"Our Final Invention: Artificial Intelligence and the End of the Human Era" by James Barrat

Discusses AI's benefits, and more critically, the potential threats that AI poses as it advances in capability.

"The Age of Em: Work, Love, and Life when Robots Rule the Earth" by Robin Hanson

Hanson speculates on a future dominated by brain-emulation technology, exploring societal and economic implications.

"The Sentient Machine: The Coming Age of Artificial Intelligence" by Amir Husain

Discusses the implications of AI from various perspectives including philosophical, societal, and future potentials.

"New Laws of Robotics: Defending Human Expertise in the Age of AI" by Frank Pasquale

This book proposes new laws to govern the development and implementation of AI technologies, aiming to protect human expertise and dignity.

"Life 3.0: Being Human in the Age of Artificial Intelligence" by Max Tegmark

This book explores the future of artificial intelligence and its impact on the universe, addressing several profound questions about AI and our future.

"Human Compatible: Artificial Intelligence and the Problem of Control" by Stuart Russell

Stuart Russell, a leading AI researcher, challenges the current AI development paradigm that focuses on the creation of intelligent machines without adequate control mechanisms.

AI Journals:

Journal of Machine Learning Research (JMLR): JMLR is an open-access journal that publishes original research papers in all areas of machine learning. It is a highly respected journal with a strong reputation for quality

Transactions on Pattern Analysis and Machine Intelligence (TPAMI): TPAMI is a publication of the Institute of Electrical and Electronics Engineers (IEEE). It covers a wide range of topics in machine learning, including computer vision, natural language processing, and robotics.

Neural Networks: Neural Networks is a journal that publishes research on artificial neural networks and related computational models. It is a good resource for staying up-to-date on the latest advances in deep learning.

Artificial Intelligence (AI): AI is the oldest journal in the field of artificial intelligence. It publishes research on a wide range of topics, including reasoning, planning, learning, and natural language processing.

International Journal of Computer Vision (IJCV): IJCV is a journal that publishes research on computer vision, which is a subfield of artificial intelligence that deals with the analysis and understanding of images and videos.

Pattern Recognition: Pattern Recognition is a journal that publishes research on pattern recognition, which is a subfield of artificial intelligence that deals with the classification of data into categories.

Proceedings of the National Academy of Sciences (PNAS): PNAS is a general science journal that occasionally publishes research on artificial intelligence. It is a good resource for staying up-to-date on the latest advances in AI that have broad scientific implications.

Quantum Computing Journals:

Physical Review X (PRX Quantum): PRX Quantum is an open-access journal from the American Physical Society (APS) that focuses on short, high-impact communications in quantum science, including quantum information, computation, and simulation.

npj Quantum Information :npj Quantum Information is an open-access journal from Nature Research that publishes original research on the theory, simulation, and experiment of quantum information processing.

Quantum Science and Technology (QST): Quantum Science and Technology (QST) is a journal published by the Institute of Physics (IOP) that covers fundamental and applied aspects of quantum science and technology.

Nature Physics (Nat Phys): Nature Physics is a journal published by Nature Research that covers significant advances across the whole spectrum of physics research, with occasional publications on quantum computing advancements.

Online Courses:

Don't bother. Use GenAI

www.ingramcontent.com/pod-product-compliance
Lightning Source LLC
Chambersburg PA
CBHW052148220526
45471CB00004B/1576